Boho Crochet

A Quantum Book

First published in the UK in 2015 by
Apple Press
74–77 White Lion Street
London N1 9PF
United Kingdom

www.apple-press.com

ISBN 978-1-84543-562-2

QUMBOCR

This book was conceived,
designed and produced by
Quantum Books Limited
6 Blundell Street
London N7 9BH
United Kingdom

Publisher: Kerry Enzor
Project Editor: Hazel Eriksson
Editor: Julie Brooke

Designer: Blanche Williams of Harper Williams Design
Photographer: Simon Pask
Technical Consultants: Carol Meldrum, Luise Roberts and Sophie Scott

Production Manager: Rohana Yusof

Printed in China by 1010 Printing International Ltd.

9 8 7 6 5 4 3

Boho Crochet

Contributing Editor: Marinke Slump

APPLE

CONTENTS

Introduction   7
The Designers   8
Project Selector   10
Crochet for the Home   13
Crochet Fashion   73
Crochet Techniques   111
Useful Information   139
Yarns Used in the Projects   140
Index   142
Acknowledgements   144

Introduction

I've always loved the bohemian style of the late 1960s and early 1970s and I cannot resist the amazing patterns and colours that were used on everything from clothing to carpets and posters to wallpaper. Crochet was an integral part of the look then, and I have been delighted to watch it come back into fashion and give me the chance to explore it myself.

For me, the bohemian style represents creativity in its purest form: the combination of amazing colours, often inspired by nature; textures and fabrics that feel amazing to the touch; and exciting stitch patterns that will rock your world.

The original bohemian, free-spirited people who founded the look and gave it a name, were thought to be unconventional. If you, like me, are one of today's boho followers, then embrace this freedom and explore the style on your own terms by giving the patterns in this book your own twist – add tassels, use your own colour palette, or use thicker or thinner hooks and yarns to maximise or minimise the designs. Make every project unique to you.

I am really proud to present this amazing collection of crochet projects. You'll find quick-and-easy makes like pillows and coasters, as well as larger, more time-consuming items such as scarves and blankets. They come from a very talented group of bloggers and crafters (see pages 8–9) who will show you a fantastic range of crochet techniques and will inject a rainbow-coloured wave of bohemian chic into your home and wardrobe.

Go wild with boho colour and see how it can inspire you on a daily basis!

The DESIGNERS

Amy Astle

Colour, crochet and anything crafty make Amy Astle of Little Doolally happy. She has been crocheting since she was ten years old: Her grandma bought her some old 1970s weekly sewing, knitting and crochet magazines from a yard sale and she has been hooked ever since. She discovered her love for yarn, surface pattern and texture while studying for a degree in textiles. Since then, her fingers have been itching to delve into the wonderful world of crochet and inspire and teach other like-minded people at www.littledoolally.com. She lives in Nottinghamshire, UK.

Annemarie Benthem

Annemarie lives in Delft in the Netherlands. She took her first crochet class in 2010 and immediately fell in love with it. There aren't many projects she hasn't tried, and although she loves to make other people's patterns, she also loves to design herself. She hopes to inspire people with her designs. You can find more designs on her blog, www.annemarieshaakblog .blogspot.com and her Etsy shop, www.etsy.com/shop /annemariesbreiblog.

Ruth Bramham

Ruth, known online as Ruthie Joy, taught herself to knit and crochet to make clothes for her son Paul when he was a baby. She lives in Lancashire, UK, along with her husband Adrian and an enormous yarn and bead stash! Taking inspiration from nature she enjoys making accessories from natural yarns such as wool, mohair and silk. She also creates jewelry from semi-precious stones, freshwater pearls and Czech glass. When not making things she loves to walk in her beloved Yorkshire Dales and Lake District. Her work can be found at www.etsy .com/uk/shop/Yarnhappiness.

Ali Campbell

Ali remembers getting hooked on crochet as a child. Today, she always has two or three projects on the go and teaches it to others. She says: 'With just one little hook and a small ball of wool this eco-friendly craft will keep you occupied like you never thought it could!' She lives in Dorset, UK. Find her online at www.gethookedoncrochet.co.uk.

Susan Carlson

Susan describes herself as a cheerful, creative, crochet designer and collector of all things colourful. She was taught to crochet as a young girl by her granny and her first project was a long scarf for her dad. Although crochet and other craftiness have always been part of her life, she channelled her energy into teaching junior high and high school sciences for many years before she picked up a hook again and her blog, Felted Button, was born. Susan loves all things colourful – especially with buttons and yarn! Her designs can be found at FeltedButton .com. She lives in Utah.

Sara Dudek

Sara started crocheting when she was 12 years old and began designing patterns soon after. She started Sans Limites Crochet (sanslimitescrochet .blogspot.co.uk) after college and has loved watching it grow. Her crochet work has taken her to craft fairs around the United States and even included designs for the non-profit company Krochet Kids International. She has an Etsy store and currently lives in Colorado where she spends her days studying design in graduate school, teaching dance and exploring the Rocky Mountains.

Carmen Heffernan

Carmen lives in the Irish countryside with her husband and their delightful dogs and cats. Her mother and aunts were all creative and skillful at needlework, so it has always been a part of her life. Carmen is passionate about crochet and colour and feels driven to create every day! She also loves to teach crochet and to inspire others to express themselves with hooks and yarn. Carmen especially loves taking simple patterns and using different or surprising colour combinations to create something vibrant and beautiful. She documents her crochet creations on Instagram, at http://instagram.com /anniedesigncrochet and sells her colourful crochet flowers on Etsy (www.etsy.com/shop /AnnieDesign).

Dorien Hollewijn

Ever since she was a little girl Dorien has been playing with yarn and fabric. Her doll had a huge wardrobe of knitted, crocheted and sewn garments. A few years ago, when circumstances kept her at home, she immediately picked up yarn and fabrics to keep her occupied. And because she learned so much about all crafts from other bloggers she started her own blog (madebydo.blogspot.nl) about her adventures in the world of fibre. Her work emphasises the possibilities of colour: she says that creating a simple square or hexagon over and again with different colours, and then arranging them into one gorgeous blanket, is the best game ever. She has an Etsy store, (www.etsy .com/uk/shop/JustDo) and lives in the Netherlands.

Sandra Paul

Sandra Paul is a craft blogger and pattern designer who loves to crochet, knit and sew. She lives in a small village in Bedfordshire, UK, with her husband, daughter and an ever-expanding stash of yarn and fabric. Re-discovering knitting as an adult by dusting off some rusty childhood skills one Christmas day, it was only a matter of weeks before she knew that she needed to learn crochet too. One how-to book and a stressful evening of fumbled fingers later, a slightly crooked granny square and a brand new obsession had been born. Her designs can be found at www.cherryheart.co.uk.

Marinke Slump

Marinke (known online as Wink) is a blogger and designer, who came to the attention of the crochet community for her colourful mandalas. She first learned to crochet from a small book on how to make amigurumi. Armed with some cotton yarn and a crochet hook that was way too small, she taught herself the double crochet stitch. Her first crochet project was supposed to become a fish, but turned out as a little pig... Now, five years later, the art of crochet feels second nature to her and she even has her dream job of being a full-time crochet blogger! Wink writes patterns on a regular basis for online and offline magazines including *Tuts+* and *Simply Crochet* and shares patterns on her blog (acreativebeing.com) and her Etsy and Ravelry shops. She lives and works from her home in the Netherlands. Find her online at acreativebeing.com.

Project
SELECTOR

Vintage Fan Ripple Blanket
Marinke Slump   **14**

Annie Blanket
Amy Astle   **16**

Daisy Baby Blanket
Carmen Heffernan   **18**

Colour Wheel Hexagon Blanket
Dorien Hollewijn   **22**

Happy Colours Blanket
Dorien Hollewijn   **25**

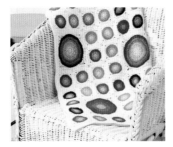

Flower Power Runner
Annemarie Benthem   **28**

Star Fruit Rug
Susan Carlson   **31**

Large Granny-Square Pillow
Carmen Heffernan   **34**

Sunflower Motif Pillow
Carmen Heffernan   **36**

Chevron Pillow
Amy Astle   **38**

Round Floor Pillow
Annemarie Benthem   **41**

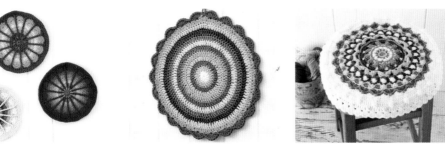

Spoke Mandala
Marinke Slump   **44**

Picot-Edge Mandala
Marinke Slump   **47**

Mandala Stool Cover
Susan Carlson   **50**

Heart and Flower Motifs
Carmen Heffernan   **57**

Crocheted Christmas Baubles
Carmen Heffernan   **60**

Butterfly Pot Holders
Marinke Slump   **63**

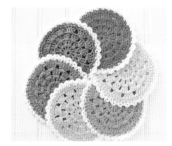

Lace Crochet Coasters
Carmen Heffernan   **66**

Breakfast Cosy Set
Carmen Heffernan   **69**

Drops of Colour Headband
Marinke Slump   **74**

Floral Hair Grips
Carmen Heffernan   **77**

Rainbow Wrist Cuffs
Sandra Paul   **78**

Slouch Hat
Marinke Slump   **83**

Dancing Hearts Wrap
Marinke Slump   **85**

Wildflowers Scarf
Ruth Bramham   **89**

Ombré String Cowl
Susan Carlson   **90**

Blossom Necklace
Ruth Bramham   **93**

Granny-Square Clutch Bag
Annemarie Benthem   **94**

**Mobile Phone and Tablet
Covers** Ali Campbell   **96**

Star Backpack
Annemarie Benthem   **100**

The Weekender Bag
Sara Dudek   **105**

Crochet for the
HOME

Cosy throws and pillows bring boho charm
to your home. Use one or two pieces to bring
a splash of colour to a sofa or easy chair –
or transform a room into a kaleidoscope of
crocheted accessories.

Vintage Fan Ripple Blanket

 **SKILL LEVEL**

This pretty pattern was inspired by a vintage design, and the simple pattern repeat means it can be easily adapted to make a smaller baby blanket or larger throw.

YOU WILL NEED

DK-weight cotton/acrylic blend yarn (approx 50 g/1.76 oz; 140 m/153 yds.)

CCa   2 balls in olive
CCb   2 balls in pink
CCc   2 balls in pale pink
CCd   2 balls in red
CCe   2 balls in violet
CCf   2 balls in yellow
CCg   2 balls in blue
Size 4 mm (US G-6) hook

Tension
Tension is not important in this project

Dimensions
Approx 140 x 140 cm (56 x 56 in.)

To make the blanket

All stitches are worked into the back loops only throughout. To make a larger or smaller blanket, start with a chain which is a multiple of 9, plus 1. Using CCa, ch280.

Row 1: 1dc into 2nd ch from hook, 1dc into next ch3, *3dc into next ch, 1dc into next ch8, rep from *, ending last rep after four of the 8dc have been worked, turn. (330sts)

Rows 2–3: ch1, *miss 1st, 1dc into next 4sts, 3dc into next st, 1dc into next 4sts, miss 1st, rep from * to end.

Row 4: sl st into first 3sts, ch6 (counts as 1qtr), 1qtr into next 2sts, 3qtr into next st, 1qtr into next 3sts, miss next 2sts, *miss next 2sts, 1qtr into next 3sts, 3qtr into next st, 1qtr into next 3sts, miss next 2sts, rep from * to end, turn.

Fasten off yarn and join in CCb.

Row 5: ch1, *1dc into next 4sts, dc3 into next st, 1dc into next 4sts, rep from * to end.

Rows 2–5 form pattern repeat. Repeat these rows, changing colour after Row 4 on each repeat as follows.

Rows 6–8: CCb.
Rows 9–12: CCc.
Rows 13–16: CCd.
Rows 17–20: CCe.
Rows 21–24: CCf.
Rows 25–28: CCg.

Repeat stripe sequence until blanket is the required size. On the last repeat do not fasten off yarn after Row 4 but repeat Rows 5, 2 and 3 to form the edge.

Finishing

Fasten off yarn and weave in loose ends. Block if required.

Annie Blanket

❋ SKILL LEVEL

Dotted stripes add a playful touch of colour to this baby blanket. You can use a different colour for each stripe, or restrict yourself to one or two.

YOU WILL NEED

DK-weight cotton yarn (approx 50 g/1.76 oz; 100 m/109 yds.)
MC   5 balls in white
CC   Scraps of yarn in 12 colours
Size 3.5 mm (US E-4) hook

Tension

18 stitches by 9 rows over 10 cm (4 in.) square using tr; however tension is not essential for this pattern

Dimensions

Approx 45 x 56 cm (21 x 24 in.)

To make the blanket

To make a larger/smaller blanket, work your chain in a number divisible by 3, plus 2.

Using MC, ch101.

Row 1: 1dc into 2nd ch from hook, 1dc into each ch to end, turn. (100sts)

Row 2: ch2 (counts as first tr), 2tr into first st, *miss 2sts, 3tr into next st, rep from * to end, turn. (34 sets of 3tr)

Fasten off MC and join in CC of choice.

Row 3: ch3 (counts as 1dc and ch2), *1dc in between next two groups of 3tr, ch2, rep from *, ending last rep with 1dc into top of ch2 at beg of previous row.

Fasten off CC and join in MC.

Row 4: ch2 (counts as first tr), 2tr into first ch2sp, *miss next st, 3tr into next ch2sp, rep from * to end.

Fasten off MC and join in CC.

Rows 3–4 form pattern. Repeat until 74 rows of pattern have been worked or until blanket is required length. Do not fasten off yarn.

Row 75: ch1, 1dc into each st to end.

Fasten off yarn and weave in loose ends.

Edging

Using MC, join yarn to any dc on last row worked.

Round 1: ch1, 1dc into same st as you joined yarn to, 1dc into each st to corner, 3dc into corner st (first corner made), work 1dc into each st down the side of the blanket to corner, 3dc into corner st (second corner made), 1dc into each st along edge to next corner, 3dc into corner st (third corner made), 1dc into each st up the side of the blanket to corner, 3dc into corner st (fourth corner made), 1dc to end, sl st into ch1 at beg of round.

Round 2: ch1, 1dc into first st, *1dc into each st to centre st of 3dc corner, 3dc into corner st, rep from * until all corners have been worked, 1dc into each st to end, sl st into ch1 at beg of round.

Round 3: as Round 2.

Fasten off yarn and weave in loose ends.

Finishing

Block if required.

Daisy Baby Blanket

SKILL LEVEL

Colourful daisies are scattered over this pretty blanket. This size is perfect for a baby's crib, but why not make a larger one for picnics?

Special stitches

tr3cluster: work as tr3tog working each tr into the same st or space to make a cluster.

tr4cluster: work as tr4tog working each tr into the same st or space to make a cluster.

To make the blanket

DAISY WHEEL SQUARE (MAKE 30)

Using CC of choice, ch5, join ends with sl st to form ring.

Round 1: ch1 (counts as first st), 11dc into ring, sl st into ch1 at beg of round. (12sts)

Round 2: ch4 (count as 1tr and ch1), *1tr into next st, ch1, rep from * to end, sl st into third of ch4 at beg of round. (12 ch1sp) Fasten off yarn.

Join in MC into any of the ch1sp from previous round.

Round 3: ch3 (counts as first st), tr3cluster into same ch1sp, ch3, *tr4cluster into next ch1sp, ch3, rep from * to end, sl st into top of first cluster. (12 clusters)

Fasten off MC and join in next CC of choice into any of the ch3sp from previous round.

Round 4: ch4 (counts as first st), work [2dtr, ch3, 3dtr] into same ch3sp (corner made), 3tr into next two ch3sp, *work [3dtr, ch3, 3dtr] into next ch3sp (corner made), 3tr into next two ch3sp, rep from * to end, sl st into top of ch4 at beg of round. (4 ch3sp)

Round 5: sl st across sts and into first ch3sp, ch3 (counts as first st), work [2tr, ch3, 3tr] into same ch3sp (corner made), [miss next 3sts, 3tr in between next 2sts (stsp)] 3 times, *work [3tr, ch3, 3tr] into next ch3sp (corner made), [miss next 3sts, 3tr into next stsp] 3 times, rep from * to end, sl st into top of ch3 at beg of round. (20 sets of 3tr)

Fasten off CC and join in MC to any of the stitches on previous round.

Round 6: ch3 (counts as first st), *1tr into each st until ch3sp, work [2tr, ch1, 2tr] into ch3sp, rep from * 3 times more, 1tr into each st to end of round, sl st into top of ch3 at beg of round. (76sts)

Round 7: ch1 (counts as first st), 1dc into each st until ch3sp, work [1dc, ch1, 1dc] into ch3sp, rep from * 3 times more, 1dc into each st to end of round, sl st into ch1 at beg of round.

Fasten off yarn and weave in loose ends.

Finishing

Lay out squares in your choice of design in six rows made up of five squares across. Using MC, hold first two squares with wrong sides together and sl st into corner space of both squares.

Ch1, 1dc into same place, work 1dc into matching sts from both squares up to next corner, 1dc into corner.

Do not break off yarn but join next two squares together as given above until five sets of two squares have been joined.

Join the next row of squares to the first row of squares. Continue joining as set until all squares have been joined.

Next join the squares vertically as given for the rows, sl st over sections where the squares are already joined.

Border

Use MC for the first and last round of border and three CC shades for Rounds 2–4 of border.

Using MC and with RS facing you, join with sl st to any st on outer edge of blanket.

Round 1: ch1, 1dc into each st and chsp until first corner, work [1dc, ch1, 1dc] into first corner, *1dc into each st and chsp to next corner**, work [1dc, ch1, 1dc] into corner, rep from *, ending last rep at **.

Fasten off MC and join first CC of choice into any st from previous round.

Round 2: ch2, 1htr into each st until first corner, work [1htr, ch1, 1htr] into first corner, *1htr into each st and chsp to next corner**, work [1htr, ch1, 1htr] into corner, rep from *, ending last rep at **.

Fasten off CC and join second CC of choice into any st from previous round.

Round 3: as Round 2.

Fasten off CC and join third CC of choice into any st from previous round.

Round 4: as Round 2.

Fasten of CC and join in MC into any st from previous round.

Round 5: ch1, 1dc into same st, ch2, 1htr into dc just worked, miss next st, *1dc into next st, ch2, 1htr into dc just worked, miss next st, rep from * to end.

Fasten off yarn and weave in loose ends.

Block if required.

Join the daisy wheel squares together to create a field of colourful blooms. Arrange the different colours in rows or place them in a random order.

Colour Wheel Hexagon Blanket

 **SKILL LEVEL**

Pinwheeling hexagons are an interesting spin on classic granny squares. But it's the colour placement, based on the colour wheel, that makes this blanket so eye-catchingly special.

YOU WILL NEED

Sport-weight cotton yarn (approx 50 g/
1.76 oz; 161 m/176 yds.)
MC   16 balls in white
CC   approx 25 g/1 oz. each of
         24 additional colours
Size 4 mm (US G-6) hook

Tension
A hexagon measures 8.5 cm (3½ in.) wide

Dimensions
148 x 142 cm (58 x 52 in.)

To make the blanket

The blanket is made with white-bordered hexagons with circles that gradually change in colour from pale colours in the centre, to darker colours around the outsides.
Start the first hexagon using the same CC for the first three rounds and the MC for the last two rounds. For the second hexagon add new CCa for first round, then complete as the first hexagon.
For the third hexagon work first two rounds using CCa and complete as first hexagon.
For the fourth hexagon work first round in CCb, the second round in CCa and the third round in CC and complete as first hexagon.

HEXAGON MOTIF (MAKE 252)

Using CC of choice, make magic loop.
Round 1: ch3 (counts as first tr), tr2tog into ring, ch3, *tr3tog, ch3, rep from * four more times, sl st into top of ch3 at beg of round. (6 clusters)
Sl st into next ch3sp.
Round 2: ch3 (counts as first tr), work [tr2tog, ch3, tr3tog] into same ch3sp, ch1, *work [tr3tog, ch3, tr3tog] into next ch3sp, ch1, rep from * to end, sl st into top of ch3 at beg of round. (12 clusters)
Sl st into next ch3sp.
Round 3: ch3 (counts as first tr), work [tr2tog, ch3, tr3tog] into same ch3sp, ch1, tr3tog into next ch1sp, *ch1, work [tr3tog, ch3, tr3tog] into next ch3sp, ch1, tr3tog into next ch1sp, ch1, rep from * to end, sl st into top of ch3 at beg of round. (18 clusters)
Fasten off yarn and join in MC.
Sl st into next ch3sp.
Round 4: ch3 (counts as first tr), work [2tr, ch2, 3tr] into same ch3sp, work [3tr into next ch1sp] twice, *work [3tr, ch2, 3tr] into next ch3sp,

work [3tr into next ch1sp] twice, rep from * to end, sl st into top of ch3 at beg of round. (24 sets of 3tr)

Round 5: ch1 (counts as first dc), work 1dc into each stitch and 2dc into each ch2sp to end, sl st into ch1 at beg of round. (84sts)

Fasten off yarn and weave in loose ends.

Finishing

Using picture as guide, keep adding hexagons, using the colour wheel as a guide. Once hexagons are completed sew or crochet together, working through the back loops only of the stitches at the outer edge.

Happy Colours Blanket

The circles of bright colours scattered over this blanket will make you smile every time you wrap yourself in its cosy stitches.

YOU WILL NEED

Sport-weight cotton yarn (approx 50 g/
1.76 oz; 161 m/176 yds.)
MC   15 balls in white
CC   Approx 2,560 m/2,800 yds. total
        of assorted colours
Size 3.5 mm (US E-4) hook

Tension

A small square measures
7 cm (2¾ in.) square
A large square measures
13.5cm (5¼ in.) square

Dimensions

99 x 160 cm (39 x 63 in.)

To make the blanket

For the small circles, the first three rounds are crocheted with different shades of the same colour; for the large circles, four shades of the same colour have been used. Start with pale colours at the centre, moving to darker colours at the outsides.

SMALL CIRCLE-IN-SQUARE MOTIF (MAKE 254)

Using lightest shade of colour of choice, make magic loop.

Round 1: ch3 (counts as first st), 11tr into ring, sl st into top of ch3 at beg of round. (12sts)
Fasten off yarn and join in next shade of same colour. Pull magic loop tight to close.

Round 2: ch3 (counts as first st), 1tr into same place as ch3, 2tr into each st to end, sl st into top of ch3 at beg of round. (24sts)
Fasten off yarn and join in next shade of same colour.

Round 3: ch3 (counts as first st), 2tr into next st, *1tr into next st, 2tr into next st, rep from * to end, sl st into top of ch3 at beg of round. (36sts)
Fasten off yarn and join in MC to any st from last round.

EDGING

Round 4: ch1 (counts as first st), 1dc into next 2sts, *1htr into next st, 1tr into next st, work [1dtr, ch1, 1dtr] into next st, 1tr into next st, 1htr into next st, 1dc into next 4sts, rep from *, ending last rep after two of the 4dc have been worked, sl st into ch1 at beg of round. (40sts)

Round 5: ch3 (counts as first st), *1tr into each st up to ch1sp, work [2tr, ch1, 2tr] into ch1sp, rep from * until four ch1sp have been worked into, 1tr into each st to end, sl st into top of ch3 at beg of round. (56sts)
Fasten off yarn and weave in the loose ends.

Large circle in square motif (make 23)

Work Rounds 1–3 as given for small circle, working first two rounds in lightest shade and third round in next shade of same colour.

Round 4: ch3 (counts as first st), 1tr into next st, 2tr into next st, *1tr into next 2sts, 2tr into next st, rep from * to end, sl st into top of ch3 at beg of round. (48sts)

Fasten off yarn and join in next shade of same colour.

Round 5: ch3 (counts as first st), 1tr into next 2sts, 2tr into next st, *1tr into next 3sts, 2tr into next st, rep from * to end, sl st into top of ch3 at beg of round. (60sts)

Round 6: ch3 (counts as first st), 1tr into next 3sts, 2tr into next st, *1tr into next 4sts, 2tr into next st, rep from * to end, sl st into top of ch3 at beg of round. (72sts)

Fasten off yarn and join in next shade of same colour.

Round 7: ch3 (counts as first st), 1tr into next 4sts, 2tr into next st, *1tr into next 5sts, 2tr into next st, rep from * to end, sl st into top of ch3 at beg of round. (84sts)

Fasten off yarn and join in MC to any st from last round.

Edging

Round 8: ch1 (counts as first st), 1dc into next 3sts, *1htr into next 2sts, 1tr into next 2sts, 1dtr into next 2sts, work [1trtr, ch1, 1trtr] into next st, 1dtr into next 2sts, 1tr into next 2sts, 1htr into next 2sts, 1dc into next 8sts, rep from *, ending last rep after four of the 8dc have been worked, sl st into ch1 at beg of round. (88sts)

Round 9: ch3 (counts as first st), *1tr into each st up to ch1sp, work [2tr, 1dtr, ch1, 1dtr, 2tr] into ch1sp, rep from * until four ch1sp have been worked into, 1tr into each st to end, sl st into top of ch3 at beg of round. (112sts)

Finishing

Using the picture as guide, start by making larger blocks by sewing two smaller blocks to one side of a larger block and three smaller blocks to the top or bottom of the larger block. Once you have made enough blocks for your blanket, either sew or crochet these together, making sure that you turn the blocks so you don't get a line of larger blocks.

Border

Join in MC to any stitch.

Round 1: ch1 (counts as first st), work 1dc into each st up to first ch1sp, work [3dc into ch1sp], *1dc into each st to next ch1sp, [3dc into next ch1sp], rep from * until all four corners have been worked, 1dc into each st to end, sl st into ch1 at beg of round.

Round 2: ch3 (counts as first st), *work 1tr into each st up to centre st of 3dc of previous round, 3tr into next st, rep from * until all four corners have been worked, 1tr into each st to end, sl st into top of ch3 at beg of round.

Fasten off yarn and weave in loose ends.

Bright colours work like a ray of sunshine, illuminating their surroundings. But the squares could be made using pastel shades for a more restful, but equally beautiful, design.

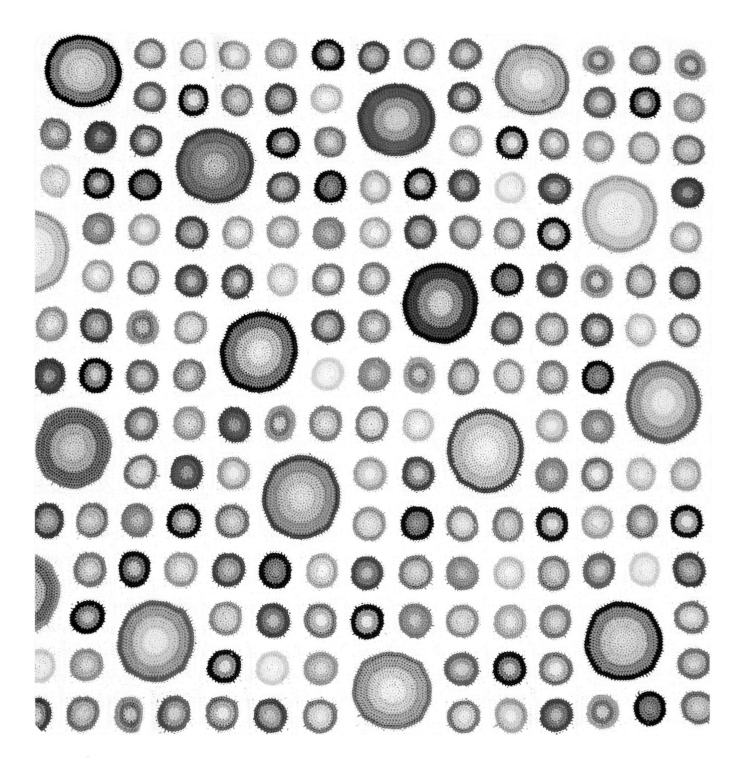

Flower Power Runner

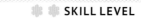

The blooms on this open-work runner will add a shot of colour to any room. Drape it over the arm or back of a sofa or chair, or arrange it in the centre of a table.

YOU WILL NEED

Aran-weight cotton yarn (approx 50 g/ 1.76 oz; 75 m/83 yds.)
MC   1 ball in vanilla
CC   Scraps of yarn in 15 assorted colours
Size 4 mm (US G-6) hook

Tension
A flower measures 7cm (2¾ in.) square

Dimensions
78 x 52 cm (30¾ x 20½ in.)

To make the blanket

THE FIRST FLOWER

Using MC, ch4, join ends with sl st to form ring.
Round 1: ch1, 8dc into ring, sl st into ch1 at beg of round. (8sts) Fasten off yarn and join in colour of choice.
Round 2: *ch8, sl st into next st, rep from * to end, working last sl st into ch1 at beg of round. (8 loops)
Round 3: dc9 into first ch8 loop, sl st into next st, *dc9 into next ch8 loop, sl st into next st, rep from * to end. Fasten off yarn.

SECOND FLOWER

Work Rounds 1–2 as for first flower. Join flowers together on the next round as follows.
Round 3: work [4dc into first ch8 loop, 1dc into fifth dc of first flower petal, 4dc into ch8 loop of second flower, sl st into next st] twice, *9dc into next ch8 loop, sl st into next st, rep from * to end. Fasten off yarn.

THIRD FLOWER

Work as given for second flower, joining fifth and sixth petals to first and second petals of previous flower. Continue working in this way until twelve flowers have been linked. First row of runner is now complete.

FIRST FLOWER OF SECOND ROW

Work as given for second flower, joining seventh and eighth petals to third and fourth petals of twelfth flower from first row.

SECOND FLOWER OF SECOND ROW

Work as given for second flower, joining fifth and sixth petals to first and second petals of previous flower and seventh and eight petals to third and fourth petals from eleventh flower from first row.

Continue working in this way until twelve flowers have been linked. Second row is now complete.

Link a further six rows of flowers in different colours.

Finishing

Weave in loose ends and block if required.

Star Fruit Rug

Bold colours bring a modern, boho touch to the star motifs on this rug. The stars are crocheted together as you work in a series of progressive sets of colours.

YOU WILL NEED

Worsted/aran-weight wool yarn (approx 100 g/3.5 oz; 142 m/155 yds.)
CC   1 skein in orange red
CCa   1 skein in red
CCb   1 skein in gold
CCc   1 skein in light green
CCd   1 skein in medium green
CCe   1 skein in turquoise
CCf   1 skein in light blue
CCg   1 skein in magenta
CCh   1 skein in dark blue
Size 4 mm (US G-6) hook

Tension
A star motif measures approx 10 cm (4 in.) across from point to point

Dimensions
Approx 94 x 61 cm (37 x 24 in.)

Special stitches
FPtr and FPdtr: tr and dtr, respectively, worked behind the post of the designated stitch on the side facing you.

Surface sl st: insert hook through designated st and draw up loop from the WS of the motif and complete sl st on the RS; insert hook into next st, draw up loop and complete sl st. Continue around the motif working into each designated st.

NOTE: each star motif requires approximately 15.5 m (17 yds.) of worsted/aran-weight yarn. If you choose to design something with different dimensions, multiply the total number of motifs by 15.5 m (17 yds.) to determine the total length of yarn required. For example, if you want to make a rug measuring 94 x 122 cm (37 x 48 in.) you will need 2 skeins of each colour.

To make the rug

First star motif
Using colour of choice, ch6, join ends with sl st to form ring.
Round 1: *ch1, work [1tr, 1dtr, 1tr, ch1, sl st] into ring, ch1, rep from * 5 more times. (6 petals)
Round 2: *ch2, miss ch1, work [FPtr into next st, FPdtr into next st, FPtr into next st, ch2], miss ch1, sl st into sl st from previous round, rep from * to end.
Round 3: *ch2, miss ch2, work [FPtr into next st, FPdtr into next st, FPtr into next st, ch2], miss ch2, 1dc into sl st from previous round, rep from * to end.
Fasten off yarn and weave in loose ends.

NOTE: the next round is worked using the surface crochet technique and a contrasting colour. The hook is used with the RS of the motif facing, but the yarn will be held at the WS of the motif.

Work the surface sl st around motif, inserting hook into the top of each designated st or sp below.

Round 4: Join contrast colour with sl st into final dc of Round 3, then work down toward the centre of the motif as follows, working down the edge of the last of the six petals.

Sl st into corresponding sp on Round 2, sl st into corresponding st of Round 1, sl st into centre of ring, *work sl st into each sp back up the right side of next petal, ending with sl st into ch2sp, sl st into blo of next 3sts**, work sl st into each sp back down left-hand side of same petal, and into loop, rep from *, ending last rep at **.

Fasten off yarn and pull tail through to WS. Weave in loose ends.

NOTE: the next round is worked into the top of the sts from Round 3; they are at the WS of the motif.

Round 5: join next colour into any sl st on Round 3, *sl st into ch2sp, 1dc into next st, work [1dc, ch3, 1dc] into next st (corner worked), 1dc into next st, sl st into next ch2sp, rep from * to end, sl st into sl st at beg of round.

SECOND STAR MOTIF

Using next set of three colours, start by working Rounds 1–4 as given for first motif.

NOTE: you will also join the motifs together as you go on next round.

Round 5: join next colour into any sl st on Round 3, *sl st into next ch2sp, 1dc into next st, work [1dc, ch1, sl st into ch3sp from first motif, ch1, 1dc] into next st (corner join worked), 1dc into next st, sl st into next ch2sp, rep from *, working corner join into two corners only for first row of motifs, for remaining corners work as for Round 5 of the first motif.

Using picture as a guide, join all the motifs together as Round 5, working into two corners from each motif.

Finishing

Work a total of seven rows, keeping the progressive sequence of colours as shown in the picture.

Weave in loose ends and block if required.

Each star fruit motif uses three colours. Create multiple colour combinations and maximum colour contrast.

Large Granny-Square Pillow

 **SKILL LEVEL**

Brightly coloured cotton yarns make a pillow ideal for sunny days.
Make a couple for your sofa or a set to use in the garden.

YOU WILL NEED

Scraps of DK-weight cotton yarn in
8 assorted colours
46 x 46 cm (18 x 18 in.) pillow in plain,
neutral colour
Size 4 mm (US G-6) hook

Tension
Each pattern repeat measures approx 1.8 cm
(¾ in.) Approx 8 rows of 4 pattern repeats
per 10 cm (4 in.) square

Dimensions
To fit 46 cm (18 in.) square pillow form

Pictured on page 35, top

To make the pillow

Using colour of choice, ch5, join
ends with sl st to form ring.
Round 1: ch3 (counts as first tr), 2tr
into ring, *ch3, 3tr into ring,
rep from * twice more, ch3, sl st
into top of ch3 at beg of round.
(4 sets of 3tr)
Fasten off yarn and join new colour
into any ch3sp.
Round 2: ch3 (counts as first tr),
work [2tr, ch3, 3tr] into same ch3sp,
*ch1, miss next 3sts, work [3tr, ch3,
3tr] into next ch3sp, rep from *
twice more, ch1, sl st into top of ch3
at beg of round. (8 sets of 3tr)
Fasten off yarn and join new colour
into any ch3sp.
Round 3: ch3 (counts as first tr),
work [2tr, ch3, 3tr] into same ch3sp,
*ch1, miss next 3sts, 3tr in ch1sp,
ch1**, work [3tr, ch3, 3tr] into next
ch3sp, rep from * 3 more times,
ending last rep at **, sl st into top of
ch3 at beg of round. (12 sets of 3tr)

Fasten off yarn and join new colour
into any ch3sp.
Round 4: ch3 (counts as first tr),
work [2tr, ch3, 3tr] into same ch3sp,
*[ch1, miss next 3sts, 3tr into ch1sp,
ch1] twice**, work [3tr, ch3, 3tr]
into next ch3sp, rep from * 3 more
times, ending last rep at **, sl st
into top of ch3 at beg of round.
(16 sets of 3tr)
Fasten off yarn and join new colour
into any ch3sp.
Repeat Round 4, keeping increases
as set, adding one set of 3tr to
each of the side sections until
approximately 17 rounds have
been worked or panel measures
approximately 43 x 43 cm
(17 x 17 in.).

Edging

Using colour of choice, join yarn
into top of any tr of Round 4.
Round 5: ch1, 1dc into same st,
work 1dc into each st and ch1sp,

work 3dc into each ch3sp, sl st into ch1 at beg of round. Fasten off yarn.

Finishing
Block panel to correct size and weave in loose ends.
Pin crochet panel to pillow, then using sharp sewing needle and matching thread, sew into place.

Sunflower Motif Pillow

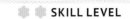

Simple granny squares build up to make a colourful, cosy pillow. Raid your yarn stash for the motif colours and choose a border colour to contrast or complement them.

YOU WILL NEED

DK-weight cotton/bamboo blend yarn (approx 100 g/3.5 oz; 230 m/250 yds.)
MC   1 ball in cream
Scraps of yarn in 4 colours for the motifs
46 x 46 cm (18 x 18 in.) pillow form
Size 3.5 mm (US E-4) hook

Tension

Each granny square measures approx 8.5 cm (3½ in.) square

Dimensions

To fit 46 cm (18 in.) square pillow form

To make the pillow

GRANNY SQUARE MOTIF (MAKE 16)
Using colour of choice, make magic loop.

Round 1: ch3 (counts as first tr), 11tr into loop, join with sl st into top of ch3 at beg of round. (12tr) Fasten off yarn. Join in colour of choice between any of the stitches.

Round 2: ch3 (counts as first tr), 1tr into same sp, *2tr into next sp, rep from * to end, sl st into top of ch3 at beg of round. (12 sets of 2tr) Fasten off yarn and join in colour of choice in between any of the sets of 2tr.

Round 3: ch3 (counts as first tr), 2tr into same sp, miss next 2sts, *3tr into next sp, miss next 2sts, rep from * to end, sl st into top of ch3 at beg of round. (12 sets of 3tr) Fasten off yarn and join in MC in between any of the sets of 3tr.

Round 4: ch3 (counts as first tr), work [2tr, ch2, 3tr] into same sp, *work [miss 3sts, 3tr into next sp] twice, miss 3sts**, work [3tr, ch2, 3tr] into next sp, rep from * 3 more times, ending last rep at **, sl st into top of ch3 at beg of round.

Round 5: ch1 (counts as first dc), 1dc into next 2sts, work 3dc into first ch2sp (first corner made), *1dc into each st to next ch2sp, work 3dc into next ch2sp (corner made), rep from * twice more, 1dc into each st to end, sl st into ch1 at beg of round. Fasten off yarn and weave in ends. Make a further 15 squares.

Finishing

Sew the squares together to make four rows of four squares.

Edging

Using MC and with RS facing, join yarn to any stitch on outer edge.

Round 1: ch3 (counts as first tr), 1tr into each st to corner, *work [2tr, ch2, 2tr] into next st (corner made), 1tr into each st to next corner, rep from * until four corners have been made, 1tr into each st to end, sl st into top of ch3 at beg of round. Repeat Round 1 until work is required size, working [2tr, ch2, 2tr] into each ch2sp to make corners. Fasten off yarn and weave in loose ends.

Block the panel so it is square. Pin crochet panel to pillow, then using sharp sewing needle and matching thread, sew into place.

Chevron Pillow

Alternating cream and coloured chevrons make a smart cover for a pillow. To make using different colours easier, use a separate ball of yarn for each chevron.

YOU WILL NEED

Aran-weight cotton yarn (approx 50 g/ 1.76 oz; 75 m/83 yds.)

MC   5 balls in off white
CCa   1 ball in gold
CCb   1 ball in vanilla
CCc   1 ball in rust
CCd   1 ball in light blue
CCe   1 ball in medium blue
CCf   1 ball in dark beige
CCg   1 ball in light pink
CCh   1 ball in moss green
40 x 40 cm (16 x 16 in.) pillow form
4 buttons, 2.5 cm (1 in.) diameter
Size 4 mm (US G-6) hook

Tension

A chevron measures 8.25 x 5 cm (50 g/ 1.76 oz; x 2 in.)

Dimensions

To fit 40 cm (16 in.) square pillow form

To make the pillow

Using MC, ch72.

Row 1: 2tr into 3rd ch from hook, 1tr into next ch3, work [tr3tog over next ch3] twice, 1tr into next ch3, 3tr into next st, *change to CC of choice, 3tr into next ch, 1tr into next ch3, work [tr3tog over next ch3] twice, 1tr into next ch3, 3tr into next ch, change to MC, 3tr into next ch, 1tr into next ch3, work [tr3tog over next ch3] twice, 1tr into next ch3, 3tr into next ch, rep from * once more, turn. (5 chevrons)

Keeping chevron block colours correct as set, work next row as follows.

Row 2: ch2 (counts as first tr), 2tr into st, *1tr into next 3sts, work [tr3tog over next 3sts] twice, 1tr into next 3sts**, work [3tr into next st] twice, rep from * 4 more times, ending last rep at **, work 3tr into top of ch2 at beg of previous row, turn.

Row 2 forms chevron pattern; repeat Row 2 twice more. Fasten off yarn.

Row 5: work as Row 2 starting with CC of choice, then MC.

Repeat Row 5 three more times. Fasten off yarn.

Keeping chevron block pattern as set, repeat until 16 sets of the four-row chevrons have been worked. On last row of final chevron do not fasten off yarn; join in MC for button band.

To make the buttonholes

Row 1: ch2 (counts as first tr), 2tr into first st, *1tr into next 3sts, work [tr3tog over next 3sts] twice, 1tr into next 3sts**, ch3, miss 2sts, rep from * 4 more times, ending last rep at **, 3tr into top of ch2 at beg of previous row, turn.

Row 2: ch2 (counts as first tr), 2tr into first st, 1tr into next 3sts, *work [tr3tog over next 3sts] twice, 1tr into next st, 8tr into ch3sp, 1tr into next

st, rep from * 3 more times, work [tr3tog over next 3sts] twice, 1tr into next 3sts, 3tr into top of ch2 at beg of previous row.
Fasten off yarn and weave in loose ends.

Finishing
Block the fabric. With WS facing, make an envelope by folding the plain edge over the buttonholed edge. Make sure that the length of your folded cover measures the same as the width to make it approx 40 cm (16 in.) square. Sew down the sides of the cover using matching yarn and back stitch. Turn RS out, making sure the corners are pointed (use a pencil to push the corner out), then sew buttons onto the plain edge to correspond with the buttonholes. Insert pillow form.

Use the photographs as a guide for placing the contrast colours, or make up your own colour pattern.

Round Floor Pillow

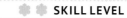 SKILL LEVEL

Simple rounds of treble crochet quickly build up into a cover for a circular pillow. The pattern is easy to adapt for any size of pillow insert – just add or subtract rounds.

YOU WILL NEED

Scraps of sport-weight cotton yarn in 7 assorted colours
35 cm (14 in.) diameter circular pillow form
Size 4 mm (US G-6) hook

Tension
21 stitches by 11 rows over 10 cm (4 in.) square using tr

Dimensions
To fit a 35 cm (14 in.) diameter pillow form

To make the pillow

FRONT PANEL

Using colour of choice, ch4, join ends with sl st to form ring.

Round 1: ch4 (counts as 1tr and ch1), *1tr into ring, ch1, rep from * 6 more times, sl st into third of ch4 at beg of round. (8 spaces)
Fasten off yarn and join colour of choice into first ch1sp.

Round 2: ch3 (counts as first tr), 1tr into same ch1sp, ch1, *2tr into next ch1sp, ch1, rep from * to end, sl st into top of ch3 at beg of round.
Fasten off yarn and join colour of choice into first ch1sp.

Round 3: ch3 (counts as first tr), work [1tr, ch1, 2tr] into same ch1sp, *work [2tr, ch1, 2tr] into each ch1sp, ch1, rep from * to end, sl st into top of ch3 at beg of round. (8 sets of 2tr, ch1, 2tr)
Fasten off yarn and join colour of choice into first ch1sp.

Round 4: ch3 (counts as first tr), 1tr into same ch1sp, *2tr into next ch1sp, rep from * to end, sl st into top of ch3 at beg of round. (16 sets of 2tr)
Fasten off yarn and join in colour of choice.

Round 5: ch3 (counts as first tr), 1tr into next st, work 1tr into each st and ch1sp to end, sl st into top of ch3 at beg of round. (48sts)
Fasten off yarn and join in colour of choice.

Round 6: ch3 (counts as first tr), 1tr into next 2sts, 2tr into next st, *1tr into next 3sts, 2tr into next st, rep from * to end, sl st into top of ch3 at beg of round. (60sts)
Fasten off yarn and join in colour of choice.

Round 7: ch3 (counts as first tr), 1tr into next 3sts, 2tr into next st, *1tr into next 4sts, 2tr into next st, rep from * to end, sl st into top of ch3 at beg of round. (72sts)
Fasten off yarn and join in colour of choice.

Round 8: ch3 (counts as first tr), 1tr into next 4sts, 2tr into next st, *1tr into next 5sts, 2tr into next st, rep from * to end, sl st into top of ch3 at beg of round. (84sts)
Fasten off yarn and join in colour of choice.
Round 9: ch3 (counts as first tr), 1tr into next 5sts, 2tr into next st, *1tr into next 6sts, 2tr into next st, rep from * to end, sl st into top of ch3 at beg of round. (96sts)
Keeping pattern and increasing as set, continue working until you have 240sts.
To ensure a snug fit, make sure the panel is slightly smaller than pillow form. Fasten off yarn and weave in loose ends.

This comfortable floor pillow is the perfect seat, whether you want to watch television, have a picnic in the garden or enjoy a good book.

BACK PANEL
Using colour of choice, ch4, join ends with sl st to form ring.
Round 1: ch3 (counts as first tr), 11tr into ring, sl st into top of ch3 at beg of round. (12sts)
Fasten off yarn and join in colour of choice.
Round 2: ch3 (counts as first tr), 1tr into same place as base of ch3, *2tr into next st, rep from * to end, sl st into top of ch3 at beg of round. (24sts)
Fasten off yarn and join in colour of choice.
Round 3: ch3 (counts as first tr), 2tr into first st, *1tr into next st, 2tr into next st, rep from * to end, sl st into top of ch3 at beg of round. (36sts)
Fasten off yarn and join in colour of choice.
Round 4: ch3, (counts as first tr), 1tr into next st, 2tr into next st, *1tr into next 2sts, 2tr into next st, rep from * to end, sl st into ch3 at beg of round. (48sts)
Fasten off yarn and join in colour of choice.

Round 5: ch3 (counts as first tr), 1tr into next 2sts, 2tr into next st, *1tr into next 3sts, 2tr into next st, rep from * to end, sl st into top of ch3 at beg of round. (60sts)
Keeping pattern and increasing as set, continue working until back panel matches front panel. Fasten off yarn and weave in loose ends.

Finishing
Sew front and back panels together as follows: place the panels together with RS facing outwards, then sew halfway around the outer edge, working through the top of the stitches. Insert the pillow form, then continue working around the outer edge. Weave in loose ends.

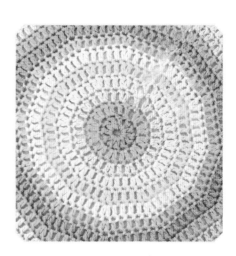

Spoke Mandala

✳ ✳ ✳ SKILL LEVEL

Crocheted mandalas – colourful disks often used as wall decorations – were originally symbolic pictures of the universe used in Tibetan Buddhism. They were designed to represent an imaginary palace that is contemplated during meditation. Each section has its own significance, representing an aspect of wisdom or reminding the meditator of a guiding principle. Many crocheters find making mandalas a therapeutic experience.

YOU WILL NEED

Scraps of worsted-weight cotton yarn in 8 assorted colours
Tapestry needle
Size 4 mm (US G-6) crochet hook
Size 4 mm (US G-6) Tunisian crochet hook

Tension
Tension is not important in this project

Dimensions
21 cm (8¼ in.) diameter

Special stitches

Standing tr: place slip knot on hook, yoh, insert hook into st, yoh and draw through (3 loops on hook), yoh and draw through first two loops (2 loops on hook), yoh and draw through last two loops (1 loop on hook).

To make the mandala

Using 4 mm hook and colour of choice, make magic loop.

Round 1: ch2 (counts as first tr), 11tr into loop. (12tr)
Pull magic loop tight to close ring. Break off yarn and pull through the loop on your hook.
Close round as follows on this and every following round.
Thread yarn through the tapestry needle and insert in the first tr you made under both loops. Pull the needle through, then insert the needle from the front to the back of the back loop of the last stitch you made. Pull the yarn gently to close round.
Join in colour of choice into blo of first stitch of previous round using standing tr technique (counts as first st).

Round 2: 1tr into blo of same st as standing tr, 2tr into blo of each st to end. (24sts)
Close round as before.
Join in colour of choice into first stitch of previous round using standing tr technique (counts as first st).

Round 3: 2tr into next st, *1tr into next st, 2tr into next st, rep from * to end. (36sts)

Close round as before.

Join in colour of choice into first st of previous round using standing tr technique (counts as first st).

Round 4: 1tr into next st, 2tr into next st, *1tr into next 2sts, 2tr into next st, rep from * to end. (48sts) Close round as before.

Join in colour of choice into first stof previous round using standing tr technique (counts as first st).

Round 5: 1tr into next 2sts, 2tr into next st, *1tr into next 3sts, 2tr into next st, rep from * to end. (60sts) Close round as before.

Join in colour of choice into first st of previous round using standing tr technique (counts as first st).

Round 6: 1tr into next 3sts, 2tr into next st, *1tr into next 4sts, 2tr into next st, rep from * to end. (72sts) Close round as before.

Join in colour of choice into first st of previous round using standing tr technique (counts as first st).

Round 7: 1tr into next 4sts, 2tr into next st, *1tr into next 5sts, 2tr into next st, rep from * to end. (84sts) Close round as before.

To make the wedges

Join in colour of choice into first st – do not use standing tr technique.

Round 8: ch1, 1dc into same st, *miss next 2sts, 6tr into next st, miss next 2sts, 1dc into next st, rep from * to end. (14 wedges) Close round as before.

To make the spokes

Using 4 mm Tunisian hook, insert hook into blo of third tr of any wedge and join in colour of choice. Extended stitches are worked into the front loops from Round 1; two of the extended stitches will need to be worked into the same front loop. Work all stitches (except extended stitches) in this round into back loops only.

Round 9: 1dc into next st, 1htr into next 2sts, 1tr into next st, make extended st as follows [yoh] 10 times (11 loops on hook), insert hook into corresponding front loop from Round 1, *yoh and draw through 2 loops, rep from * until 1 loop left on hook], **1htr into next 2sts, 1dc into next 2sts, 1htr into next 2sts, 1tr into next st, make extended st as before, rep from ** until 14 extended sts have been worked, 1htr into next st, 1dc into last st. (14 extended sts) Close round as before.

Finishing

Using 4 mm hook and same colour as previous round, join into first st of previous round using standing tr technique (counts as first st).

Round 10: 1tr into each st to end. (98sts) Fasten off yarn. Weave in loose ends.

Picot-Edge Mandala

Mandalas are a great way to use up scraps of yarn. They also allow you to experiment by combining different colours to discover the effects you can create.

YOU WILL NEED

Scraps of worsted-weight cotton yarn in 12 assorted colours
Tapestry needle
Size 4 mm (US G-6) hook

Tension
Tension is not important in this project

Dimensions
30 cm (12 in.) diameter

Special stitches
Standing tr: place slip knot on hook, yoh, insert hook into st, yoh and draw through (3 loops on hook), yoh and draw through first two loops (2 loops on hook), yoh and draw through last two loops (1 loop on hook)

Pictured on pages 48–49

To make the mandala

Using colour of choice, make a magic loop.

Round 1: ch2 (counts as first tr), 11tr into ring. (12tr)

Pull magic loop tight to close ring. Break off yarn and pull through the loop on your hook. Close round as follows on every round.

Thread yarn through the tapestry needle and insert in the first tr you made under both loops.

Pull the needle through, then insert the needle from the front to the back of the back loop of the last stitch you made. Pull the yarn gently to close round.

Join in colour of choice into blo of first st of previous round using standing tr technique (counts as first st).

Round 2: 1tr into same st as standing tr, 2tr into each st to end. (24sts)

Close round as before.

Join in colour of choice into first st of previous round using standing tr technique (counts as first st).

Round 3: 2tr into next st, *1tr into next st, 2tr into next st, rep from * to end. (36sts)

Close round as before.

Join in colour of choice into first st of previous round using standing tr technique (counts as first st).

Round 4: 1tr into next st, 2tr into next st, *1tr into next 2sts, 2tr into next st, rep from * to end. (48sts)

Close round as before.

Join in colour of choice into first st of previous round using standing tr technique (counts as first st).

Round 5: 1tr into next 2sts, 2tr into next st, *1tr into next 3sts, 2tr into next st, rep from * to end. (60sts)

Close round as before.

Join in colour of choice into first st of previous round using standing tr technique (counts as first st).

Mandalas are versatile objects - use them as wall decorations, coasters, pot holders or to line baskets. Use a large hook and chunky yarn to make rug-sized mandalas or a slim hook and lace-weight yarn to make miniature mandalas to use as gift tags.

Round 6: 1tr into next 3sts, 2tr into next st, *1tr into next 4sts, 2tr into next st, rep from * to end. (72sts) Close round as before.

Join in colour of choice into first st of previous round using standing tr technique (counts as first st).

Round 7: 1tr into next 4sts, 2tr into next st, *1tr into next 5sts, 2tr into next st, rep from * to end. (84sts) Close round as before.

Join in colour of choice into first st of previous round using standing tr technique (counts as first st).

Round 8: 1tr into next 5sts, 2tr into next st, *1tr into next 6sts, 2tr into next st, rep from * to end. (96sts) Close round as before.

Join in colour of choice into first st of previous round using standing tr technique (counts as first st).

Round 9: 1tr into next 6sts, 2tr into next st, *1tr into next 7sts, 2tr into next st, rep from * to end. (108sts) Close round as before.

Join in colour of choice into first st of previous round using standing tr technique (counts as first st).

Round 10: 1tr into next 7sts, 2tr into next st, *1tr into next 8sts, 2tr into next st, rep from * to end. (120sts) Close round as before.

Join in colour of choice into first st of previous round using standing tr technique (counts as first st).

Round 11: 1tr into next 8sts, 2tr into next st, *1tr into next 9sts, 2tr into next st, rep from * to end. (132sts) Close round as before.

Join in colour of choice into first st of previous round using standing tr technique (counts as first st).

To make the edging and loop

Join in colour of choice to first st – do not use standing tr technique.

Round 12: ch1, 1dc into same st, *miss next 2sts, 6tr into next st, miss next 2sts, 1dc into next st, rep from * to end, sl st into ch1 at beg of round. (22 fans)

Join yarn for loop as follows: insert hook into first stitch, yoh and draw through, 1dc into same st, ch10, 1dc into same st.

Fasten off yarn and weave in loose ends.

Finishing

Block if required.

The treble crochet stitch is versatile, easy to master and quick to work.

Mandala Stool Cover

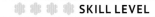 **SKILL LEVEL**

A three-dimensional mandala with a teardrop edging makes a perfect cover for a circular stool or chair seat.

Special stitches

Surface slip stitch (surf sl st): insert hook RS facing through designated stitch or space. Pull up loop from behind the work, insert into next st or space, pull up loop from behind and complete slip stitch. Insert hook into next st or space and continue slip-stitching around. Fasten off. Pull ends through to back and weave in.

tr3 cluster (tr3cl): work [yoh, insert hook through st, yoh, pull back through st, yoh, pull through 2 loops on hook] 3 times, yoh, pull through all 4 loops on hook.

tr4 popcorn (tr4pop): tr4 in same st, remove hook from loop, insert hook through first tr and into loop, yoh, pull through loop and st on hook.

tr3 popcorn (tr3pop): tr3 in same st, remove hook from loop, insert hook through first tr and back into loop, yoh and pull through loop and st on hook.

standing tr: place slip knot on hook, yoh, insert hook into st, yoh and draw through (3 loops on hook), yoh and draw through first two loops (2 loops on hook), yoh and draw through last two loops (1 loop on hook).

Picot: ch3, sl st in first ch.

To make the stool cover

This mandala is crocheted in the round with RS facing you. Each round is started by joining with a new colour and then fastened off at the end of each round unless otherwise noted. Join with standing stitches at the beginning of each round. Alternatively, join with a sl st and raise your stitches using chains; this will count as your first stitch.

NOTE: many of the rounds are worked in two parts; the first part of the round is indicated with A and the second part of the round or the surface embellishment with B.

Using CCj, make magic loop.

Round 1A: ch4 (counts as 1tr and ch1), *1tr into ring, ch1, rep from * 10 more times, sl st into third of ch4 at beg of round. (12tr)

Pull magic loop tight to close ring. Break off yarn and pull through loop on your hook. Close round as follows on this and every following round. Thread yarn through the tapestry needle and insert in the first tr you made under both loops. Pull the needle through, then insert the needle from the front to the back of the back loop of the last stitch you made.

Pull the yarn gently to close round.

Round 1B: Using CCb, work a surface sl st between the posts of the stitches of round just worked, join with sl st into first sl st. (12sl sts)

Break off yarn. Close round as before.

Using standing tr technique, join CCe into any of the ch1sp of Round 1A (counts as first st).

Round 2A: ch1, *1tr into next ch1sp, ch1, rep from * to end.

Break off yarn and close as before.

The next round is worked into the top of the stitches from Round 1A,

behind the stitches of the round just worked.

Using standing tr technique, join yarn CCf into any of the stitches from Round 1A (counts as first st).

Round 2B: ch1, *1tr into next st, ch1, rep from * to end.

Break off yarn and close as before.

The next round is worked into the ch1sp of Rounds 2A and 2B.

Add or subtract rounds from the pattern to create a mandala cover to fit your stool.

Using standing tr technique, join CCm into any of the ch1sp from Rounds 2A and 2B (counts as first st).

Round 3A: 2tr into same ch1sp, ch1, *3tr into next ch1sp, ch1, rep from * to end. (12 sets of 3tr)

Close round as before.

Round 3B: Using CCa, work a surface sl st between each stitch of round just worked, join with sl st into first sl st. (36 sl sts)

Using standing tr technique, join

CCd into any of the ch1sp from Round 3A (counts as first st).

Round 4A: tr2cl into same ch1sp, ch3, *tr3cl into next ch1sp, ch3, rep from * to end. (12 tr3cl)

Close round as before.

This next round is worked into Round 4A and Round 3A.

Join CCc into the left-hand side of any of the ch3sp next to a tr3cl with a sl st.

Round 4B: 1dc into ch3sp, *1dc into top of tr3cl, 1dc into next ch3sp, work [tr4pop] into centre stitch of 3tr from Round 3A, 1dc into same ch3sp, rep from * to end.

Close round as before.

Join CCm into top of any of the tr4pop from Round 4B with a sl st.

Round 5: 1dc into same st as sl st, ch4, *1dc into top of next tr4pop, ch4, rep from * to end.

Close round as before.

Join CCk using standing tr technique into any of the ch4sp from Round 5 (counts as first st).

Round 6A: 4tr into same ch4sp, ch1, *5tr into next ch4sp, ch1, rep from * to end. (12 sets of 5tr)

Close round as before.

Round 6B: Using CCh, work a surface sl st into top of each st and ch1sp of Round 6A, join with sl st into first sl st. (72sts)

This next round is worked into the top of the stitches from Round 6A behind the sl sts from Round 6B. Join CCg into ch1sp from Round 6A using standing tr technique (counts as first st).

Round 7A: ch3, *miss next 2sts, 1tr into next st, ch3, miss next 2sts, 1tr into next ch1sp, ch3, rep from * 10 more times, miss next 2sts, 1tr into next st, miss next 2sts, ch3, sl st into top of first st.

Do not break off yarn.

This next round is worked around the posts of stitches from Round 7A to create a wave effect.

Round 7B: *With RS facing, work 5tr around post of next st, then 5tr around post of next st back up toward outer edge, rep from * to end.

Close round as before.

This next round is worked into the ch3sp from Round 7A.

Join CCi with sl st into any of the ch3sp from Round 7A.

Round 8: *work [1dc, 1htr, 1tr, 1htr, 1dc] into next ch3sp (scallop worked), rep from * to end. (24 scallops)

Close round as before.

Join CCl into 1dc at the right-hand side of any of the scallops using standing tr technique (counts as first st).

Round 9A: 1tr into next st, ch4, *miss next 3sts, 1tr into next 2sts, ch4, rep from * to end.
Close round as before.
The next round is worked into the sts of Round 9A and around the posts of stitches in Round 8 behind the ch4sp.
Join CCm with sl st into first of the tr2 on Round 9A.
Round 9B: *1dc into each of the next 2sts of Round 9A, then work 1FPtr into next st of Round 8 scallop, 2FPtr into next st, 1FPtr into next st, rep from * to end.
Close round as before.
The next round is worked into the top of the sts from Round 9B and the ch4sp of Round 9A.
Join CCj using standing tr technique into first of 2tr in Round 9B (counts as first st).
Round 10A: 1tr into next st, 1dc into next ch4sp from Round 9A, *2tr into next 2sts from Round 9B, 1dc into next ch4sp from Round 9A, rep from * to end.
Close round as before.
The next round is worked into the top and around the base of the sts from Round 10A.
Join CCb into the right-hand side of 1dc from Round 10A.
Round 10B: ch5, *sl st in between next 2sts, sl st into base of next 4sts

from Round 10A, sl st into space at the left-hand side of next st**, ch5, rep from *, ending last rep at **. Close round as before.

The next round is worked into the top of the stitches from Round 10A and the popcorns are worked into the st to the back of the ch5 loops of Round 10B.

> *Make time to check the stitches you are working into on each round.*

Join CCe into blo of first tr stitch from Round 10A with a sl st.

Round 11: *1dc into blo of next 4sts, tr3pop into next st, push popcorn just worked through the ch5 loop from Round 10B, rep from * to end. (24 popcorns)
Close round as before.

The next round is worked into the blo of stitches on Round 11 and the back loop of centre ch of ch5 from round 10B.

Join CCf into back of third ch of ch5 from Round 10B and popcorn from Round 11.

Round 12A: miss next st, *4tr into blo of next 2sts, miss next st**, sl st into third of next ch5 and back of next popcorn, rep from *, ending last rep at **. (24 scallops)
Close round as before.

Join CCa with sl st into top of popcorn join from Round 12A.

Round 12B: *sl st into next 4 stsp, ch3, sl st into base of ch just worked (picot made), sl st into next 4 stsp, rep from * to end. (24 picots)
Close round as before. Mandala stool top section is now complete. Fasten off yarn and weave in loose ends.

Edging

Join CCm into blo of st behind picot with sl st.
Work into blo for these next rounds throughout.

Round 13: *1htr into next 2sts, 1tr into next st, tr2tog working first tr into next st, miss sl st and work second tr into next st, 1tr into next st, 1htr into next 2sts, sl st into back of next picot, rep from * to end, sl st into sl st at beg of round.

Round 14: ch3 (counts as first st), miss next st, 1tr into next 5sts, tr2tog over next st and sl st behind picot, *1tr into next 6sts, tr2tog over next st and picot, rep from * to end, sl st into top ch3 at beg of round. (24 decreases)

Round 15: ch3 (counts as first st), 1tr into each st to first decrease, tr3pop into next st, *1tr into each st to next decrease, tr3pop into next st, rep from * to end, sl st into top of ch3 at beg of round. (24 popcorns)

Round 16: ch3 (counts as first st), 1tr into each st to end, sl st into top of ch3 at beg of round.

Round 17: ch3, 1tr into next 2sts, *miss next st, 1FPtr around next st, 1FPtr around missed st, 1tr into next 5sts, rep from *, ending last rep with 1tr into last 2sts, sl st into top of ch3 at beg of round.

Round 18: ch3 (counts as first st), 2tr into same place as join, miss next 2sts, *3tr into next st, miss 2sts, rep from * to end, sl st into top of ch3 at beg of round. (56 3tr)

Round 19: *ch3, miss next 3sts, sl st in between next 2sts, rep from * to end, sl st into top of ch3 at beg of round. (56 ch3)

Round 20: work [1dc, 1htr, 1tr, 1htr, 1dc] into each ch3sp to end, sl st into 1dc at beg of round.

Finishing

Fasten off and weave in ends.

Heart and Flower Motifs

Pretty heart and flower motifs are a great way to use up scraps of yarn to make individual decorations or to complete the wreath shown on page 59. Work each flower as given in different colour combinations.

YOU WILL NEED

Scraps of sport-weight cotton yarn in variety of colours
Size 2.75 mm (US C-2) hook

Tension
Tension is not important in this project

Dimensions
Daisy approx 5.5 x 5.5 cm (2¼ x 2¼ in.)
Heart approx 6 cm (2½ in.) high

To make a heart (see page 58, top)

Using MC of choice, ch2.

Row 1: 3dc into 2nd ch from hook, turn. (3sts)

Row 2: ch1, 2dc into first st, 1dc into next st, 2dc into last st, turn. (5sts)

Row 3: ch1, 2dc into first st, 1dc into next 3sts, 2dc into last st, turn. (7sts)

Rows 4–6: ch1, 1dc into each st to end, turn.

Row 7: sl st into first st, 5tr into next st, sl st into next 3sts, 5tr into next st, sl st into last st, do not turn (10sts)

With RS facing, continue in rounds as follows.

Round 8: ch1, work 5dc down toward point, work [1dc, 1htr, 1dc] into point, work 8dc evenly up the side until you reach the third st of the 5tr from previous row, work 3dc into next st, 1dc into next 2sts, sl st into next st, miss next st, sl st into next st, 1dc into next 2sts, 3dc into next st, 1dc into next 3sts, sl st into ch1 at beg of round. (28sts)

Fasten off yarn and join in CC to any stitch from previous round. Work into each stitch as follows: *ch2, sl st into next st, rep from * to end.

Fasten off yarn and weave in loose ends.

To make a daisy (see page 58, centre)

Using colour of choice, ch4 (counts as ch1 and 1tr).

Round 1: 11tr into 4th ch from hook, sl st into top of initial ch4. (12sts)

Fasten off yarn and join in colour of choice to any st from previous round.

Round 2: ch1, 1dc into same st as you joined yarn into, 2dc into next st, *1dc into next st, 2dc into next

Glue or stitch the flowers to an embroidery hoop to make a summery wreath. The possibilities for making motifs are endless: substitute colours, layer motifs, extend the patterns to make more rounds, or add a couple of chain stitches between the outer 1tr to make pointed rather than round petal shapes.

st, rep from * to end, sl st into ch1 at beg of round. (18sts)
Fasten off yarn and join in colour of choice to any st from previous round.
Round 3: ch2, 1tr into same st, 1tr into next st, *ch2, sl st into next st, ch2, 1tr into same st as sl st just worked, 1tr into next st, rep from * to end, ch2, sl st into base of ch2 at beg of round. (9 petals)
Fasten off yarn and weave in loose ends. Block if required.

To make seven-petal flower (see below left)
Using colour of choice, ch4 (counts as ch1 and 1tr).
Round 1: 13tr into 4th ch from hook, sl st into top of initial ch4. (14sts)
Fasten off yarn and join in colour of choice to any st from previous round.
Round 2: ch1, 1dc into same st as you joined yarn into, 2dc into next

st, *1dc into next st, 2dc into next st, rep from * to end, sl st into ch1 at beg of round. (21sts)
Fasten off yarn and join in colour of choice to any st from previous round.
Round 3: ch1, 1dc into same st as you joined yarn into, 1dc into next st, 2dc into next st, *1dc into next 2sts, 2dc into next st, rep from * to end, sl st into ch1 at beg of round. (28sts)
Fasten off yarn and join in colour of choice to any st from previous round.
Round 4: ch2, 1tr into next 4sts, *ch2, sl st into next st, ch2, 1tr into same st as sl st just worked, 1tr into next 3sts, rep from * to end, ch2, sl st into base of ch2 at beg of round. (7 petals)

Finishing
Fasten off yarn and weave in loose ends. Block if required.
Work each flower as given in different colour combinations.

Crocheted Christmas Baubles

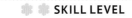 **SKILL LEVEL**

You'll want to make lots of these colourful decorations, perfect for a handmade Christmas gift or to adorn your own boho tree.

YOU WILL NEED

Scraps of DK-weight cotton yarn in 4 assorted colours for each ball
7.6 cm (3 in.) diameter Christmas ball
Size 3.5 mm (US E-4) hook

Tension
Tension is not important in this project

Dimensions
To fit purchased 7.6 cm (3 in.) diameter Christmas ball

To make a ball (make 2)

Using first colour, make magic loop.
Round 1: ch3 (counts as first tr), tr11 into loop, join with a sl st into top of ch3 at beg of round. (12sts) Pull loop tight to close opening. Fasten off yarn and join in colour of choice in between any of the sts from previous round.
Round 2: ch3 (counts as first tr), 1tr into same space as ch3, 2tr into each space to end, sl st into top of ch3 at beg of round. (24sts) Fasten off yarn and join in colour of choice in between any of the sets of 2tr of previous round.
Round 3: ch3 (counts as first tr), 2tr into same space as ch3, miss next 2sts, *3tr into next space, rep from * to end, sl st into top of ch3 at beg of round. (36sts) Fasten off yarn and join in colour of choice in between any of the sets of 3tr of previous round.
Rounds 4–5: ch3 (counts as first tr), 2tr into same space as ch3, miss next 3sts, *3tr into next space, rep from * to end, sl st into top of ch3 at beg of round. (36sts) Fasten off yarn and join in colour of choice into any of the sts from previous round.
Round 6: ch1, 1dc into same st as ch1, 1dc into each st to end, sl st into ch1 at beg of round. (36sts) Fasten off yarn and weave in loose ends.

Finishing

Once both sections of the ball have been completed, slip both pieces onto your Christmas ball, making sure that the RS are facing out, and sew together, leaving a space for the hanging loop of the ball. Fasten off yarn and weave in loose ends.

Butterfly Pot Holders

❉ ❉ ❉ **SKILL LEVEL**

Bring a burst of colour and a touch of summer to your kitchen with these butterfly-shaped pot holders. Each wing is made up of two disks that are crocheted together.

YOU WILL NEED

Scraps of DK-weight cotton yarn in
7 assorted colours
Size 4 mm (US G-6) hook

Tension

Tension is not important in this project

Dimensions

18.5 cm (7¼ in.) high

To make a butterfly mandala

THE DROPS (MAKE 4)

Using colour of choice, make a magic loop.

Round 1: ch3 (counts as first st), work [1dtr, 17tr, 1dtr, 1trtr] into ring, sl st into top of ch3 at beg of round. (21sts)
Fasten off yarn and join in colour of choice to trtr of previous round.

Round 2: ch4 (counts as 1tr and ch1), 1tr into same st, 1tr into next 10sts, 2tr into next st, 1tr into each st to end, sl st into third of ch4 at beg of round. (23sts)
Fasten off yarn and join in colour of choice to the second stitch of the 2tr at the rounded edge of drop.

Round 3: ch3 (counts as first tr), 1tr into same st, 1tr into next 3sts, 2tr into next 3sts, 1tr into next 3sts, 2tr into next st, work [1dtr, ch1, 1dtr] into chsp of beg ch of round 2, 2tr into next st, 1tr into next 3sts, 2tr into next 3sts, 1tr into next 4sts, 2tr into last st, sl st into top of ch3 at beg of round. (35sts)
Fasten off yarn.

To join the drops

Using picture as guide, lay out the droplets with all the points toward the centre.
Join in colour of choice to the st next to sl st of previous round.

Round 4: ch3 (counts as first tr), 1tr into same st, *2tr into next 2sts, 1tr into next 9sts, tr4tog over next 2sts of first drop and matching 2sts from second drop (drops joined), now work on second drop, 1tr into next 10sts, 2tr into next 3sts, 1tr into next 2sts, 2tr into next 3sts, 1tr into next 4sts, tr4tog over next 2sts of second drop and matching 2sts from third drop (drops joined), 1tr into next 5sts, 2tr into next 3sts, 1tr into next 2sts**, 2tr into next st, rep from *, ending last rep at **, sl st into top of ch3 at beg of round. (121sts) Fasten off yarn and join in colour of choice to the st just before sl st of previous round.

Round 5: ch3 (counts as first st), 1tr into same st, *1tr into next 6sts, 2tr into next 3sts, 1tr into next 5sts, tr3tog over next 3sts, 1tr into next 5sts, 2tr into next 3sts, 1tr into next 7sts, 2tr into next 2sts, 1tr into next 9sts, tr3tog over next 3sts, 1tr into next 10sts, 2tr into next 2sts, rep from *, ending last rep after first of the last two 2tr.

Fasten off yarn and join in colour of choice into the first tr st of the third increase (2tr) of the previous round.

Round 6: ch1 (counts as first dc), 1dc into next 5sts, *dc3tog over next 3sts, 1dc into next 14sts, 1htr into next 3sts, 2tr into next st, work [1tr, 1dtr] into next st, ch1, work [1dtr, 1tr] into next st, 2tr into next st, 1htr into next 3sts, 1dc into next 5sts, dc3tog over next 3sts, 1dc into next 6sts, 1htr into next 3sts, 2tr into next st, work [1tr, 1dtr] into next st, ch1, work [1dtr, 1tr] into next st, 2tr into next st, 1htr into next 3sts, 1dc into next 13sts, rep from * once more, ending last rep after 1dc has been worked into 7sts.

Fasten off yarn and join in colour of choice to the last htr worked on the previous round.

Round 7: ch1 (counts as first dc), *1dc into next 12sts, dc3tog over next 3sts, 1dc into next 14sts, 1htr into next 3sts, 1tr into next 3sts, work [2dtr, ch1, 2dtr] into ch1sp, 1tr into next 3sts, 1htr into next 3sts, 1dc into next 14sts, 1htr into next 3sts, 1tr into next 3sts, work [2dtr, ch1, 2dtr] into ch1sp, 1tr into next 3sts, 1htr into next 3sts **, 1dc into next st, rep from * to **, sl st into ch1 at beg of round. (150sts)

NOTE: on the next round you will join the centre sections of Round 3 using the same colour used for Round 3.

Round 8: insert hook into ch1sp of the bottom left droplet, join yarn with sl st, 1dc into same ch1sp, *tr4tog working first two tr into 2sts from same droplet and second two into corresponding sts from next droplet, 1dc into ch1sp of the same droplet as the last two tr worked, rep from * to end, sl st into 1dc at beg of round.

Fasten off yarn and weave in loose ends.

Finishing

With WS of pot holder facing you, using same yarn as Round 8, sew the remaining centre openings closed. Block if required.

Take time to make sure that your tension is consistent on each section - otherwise the wings will not be symmetrical.

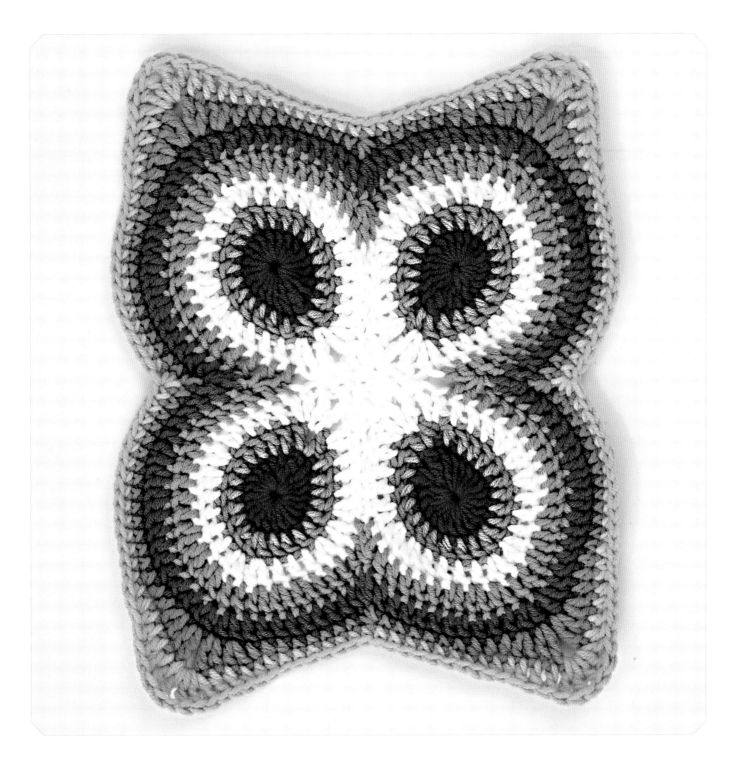

Lace Crochet Coasters

SKILL LEVEL

Graduated shades of the same colour make a pretty set of coasters with a contrasting trim. Or mix things up and use as many different colours as you like to make as many coasters as you need.

YOU WILL NEED

Scraps of worsted-weight cotton yarn in
6 graduated colours
Scraps of sport-weight cotton yarn in
1 colour for edging
Size 3.5 mm (US E-4) hook
Size 2.25 mm (US B-1) hook

Tension
Tension is not important in this project

Dimensions
approx 12 cm (4¾ in.) diameter

To make a coaster (make 6)

Using 3.5 mm hook and colour of choice, ch4, join ends with sl st to form ring.

Round 1: ch3 (counts as first tr), 11tr into ring, join with sl st into top of ch3 at beg of round. (12sts)

Round 2: sl st into next sp between tr of previous round, ch3 (counts as first tr), 1tr into same sp, *miss next st, 2tr into next sp, rep from * to end, sl st into top of ch3 at beg of round. (24sts)

Round 3: sl st across next sts and into next sp, ch3 (counts as first st), 2tr into same sp, ch1, *miss 2sts, 3tr into next sp, ch1, rep from * to end, sl st into top of ch3 as beg of round. (36sts)

Round 4: sl st across next 2sts and into next ch1sp, ch3 (counts as first st), 3tr into same sp, ch1, *miss 3sts, 4tr into next ch1sp, ch1, rep from * to end, sl st into top of ch3 at beg of round. (48sts)

Round 5: ch1 (counts as first dc), 1dc into each st and ch1sp to end, sl st into ch1 at beg of round. (60sts) Fasten off yarn.

Using the smaller 2.25 mm hook and edging yarn, join yarn to any st of previous round.

Round 6: ch1, 1dc into first st, ch2, 1htr into base of dc just worked, miss next st, *work [1dc, ch2, 1htr] into base of dc just worked, miss next st, rep from *, ending last rep with sl st into ch1 at beg of round. Fasten off yarn. Weave in loose ends.

Finishing

Block if required.
Make five more in different colours.

Breakfast Cosy Set

SKILL LEVEL

Brighten up the breakfast table with a set of granny-square cosies for your cafetière and coffee mugs; maybe even add a set of coordinating coasters.

YOU WILL NEED

Scraps of worsted-weight cotton yarn in 5 assorted colours
2 buttons 18 mm (¾ in.) diameter for Cafetière
1 button 18 mm (¾ in.) diameter for mug cosy
Size 4 mm (US G-6) hook

Tension
Tension is not important in this project

Dimensions
Cafetière cosy 21 cm (8½ in.) high
Coaster 10 cm (4 in.) square
Mug cosy 21 x 10 cm (8½ x 4 in.)

To make the cafetière cosy

GRANNY SQUARE (MAKE 2)

Using colour of choice, ch5, join ends with sl st to form ring.

Round 1: ch3 (counts as first tr), 2tr into ring, *ch3, 3tr into ring, rep from * twice more, ch3, sl st into top of ch3 at beg of round. (4 sets of 3tr)

Fasten off yarn and join new colour into any of the ch3sp.

Round 2: ch3 (counts as first tr), work [2tr, ch3, 3tr] into same ch3sp, *ch1, miss next 3sts, work [3tr, ch3, 3tr] into next ch3sp, rep from * twice more, ch1, sl st into top of ch3 at beg of round. (8 sets of 3tr)

Fasten off yarn and join new colour into any of the ch3sp.

Round 3: ch3 (counts as first tr), work [2tr, ch3, 3tr] into same ch3sp, *ch1, miss next 3sts, 3tr in ch1sp, ch1**, work [3tr, ch3, 3tr] into next ch3sp, rep from * 3 more times, ending last rep at **, sl st into top of ch3 at beg of round. (12 sets of 3tr)

Fasten off yarn and join new colour into any of the ch3sp.

Round 4: ch3 (counts as first tr), work [2tr, ch3, 3tr] into same ch3sp, *[ch1, miss next 3sts, 3tr into ch1sp, ch1] twice**, work [3tr, ch3, 3tr] into next ch3sp, rep from * 3 more times, ending last rep at **, sl st into top of ch3 at beg of round. (16 sets of 3tr)

Fasten off yarn and join new colour into any of the ch3sp.

Round 5: ch3 (counts as first tr), work [2tr, ch3, 3tr] into same ch3sp, *[ch1, miss next 3sts, 3tr into ch1sp, ch1] 3 times**, work [3tr, ch3, 3tr] into next ch3sp, rep from * 3 more times, ending last rep at **, sl st into top of ch3 at beg of round. (20 sets of 3tr)

Weave in loose ends, then sew the two squares together using same colour as the outer edge along one side.

Finishing

With RS facing you and using colour of choice, join yarn to first st after top right ch2sp edge as follows.

Round 1: ch1 (counts as first dc), 1dc into each st, ch1sp and seam to next corner, work [3dc into ch3sp, 1dc into each st and ch1sp to next corner] twice, 3dc into next ch3sp, ch11 (button loop made), 1dc into next 17sts, ch11, 1dc into next st, 3dc into last ch3sp, join with sl st into ch1 at beg of round.

Fasten yarn and weave in loose ends. Sew buttons onto RS at the opposite side from button loops.

To make the coaster

GRANNY SQUARE (MAKE 1)

Work Rounds 1–4 as given for Cafetière cosy. Fasten off yarn and weave in loose ends.

Using colour of choice, join yarn to any stitch from previous round and work edge as follows.

Round 5: ch1 (counts as first dc), 1dc into each st and ch1sp to first corner, *work 3dc into ch3sp, 1dc into each st and ch1sp to next corner, rep from * twice more, 3dc into last ch3sp, 1dc into each st to end, sl st into ch1 at beg of round. Fasten off yarn. Weave in loose ends.

To make the mug cosy

GRANNY SQUARE (MAKE 2)

Work Rounds 1–3 as given for Cafetière cosy. Fasten off yarn.

Using colour of choice, join yarn to any stitch from previous round and work edge as follows.

Round 4: ch1 (counts as first dc), 1dc into each st, ch1sp and seam to first corner, *work 3dc into ch3sp, 1dc into each st and ch1sp to next corner, rep from * twice more, 3dc into last ch3sp, 1dc into each st to end, sl st into ch1 at beg of round. Weave in loose ends. Sew the two squares together using same colour as the outer edge along one side.

Finishing

Make strap as follows.

With RS facing and granny squares lying vertically, join colour of choice to first st after 3dc into ch3sp at the top right-hand corner.

Row 1: ch1, 1dc into same st, 1dc into next 8sts, turn. (9sts)

Rows 2–6: ch1, 1dc into each st to end, turn.

Wrap cosy around mug to see if you need any extra rows and add here if required.

Row 7: ch1, 1dc into next 3sts, ch3, miss next 3sts, 1dc into each st to end. Fasten off yarn.

Round 1: ch1 (counts as first dc), *1dc into each st to centre of 3dc from round 4 of the motif, 2dc into next st, rep from * 3 more times, work 1dc into each st along edge and across the top of the strap to ch3sp, 3dc into ch3sp, 1dc into each st to end of round, sl st into ch1 at beg of round.

Fasten off yarn and weave in loose ends. Sew button onto opposite edge from strap.

Crochet FASHION

Boho crochet fashion accessories are fun to wear and a great way to add colour to your wardrobe. Keep the look subdued with a simple hairband or necklace, or make a statement with a shawl or scarf.

Drops of Colour Headband

SKILL LEVEL

The shapes that make up this cascading drops headband are
super easy to make and highly addictive.

YOU WILL NEED

Scraps of Aran-weight cotton yarn in
8 assorted colours
Headband
Hot-glue gun
Size 5 mm (US H-5) hook, or you can use a
hook one size smaller for sturdier drops

Tension
Tension is not important in this project

Dimensions
A drop measures 4 x 3.5 cm (1½ x 1¼ in.)

To make the headband
THE DROPS (MAKE 8)
Using colour of choice, make
magic loop.
Round 1: ch3 (counts as first tr),
work [1tr1, 17dc, 1tr, 1dtr, 1trtr] into
loop, join with sl st into top of ch3 at
beg of round. (22sts)
Pull loop tight and weave in
loose ends.
Make a further 7 drops using each
of the colours.

Finishing
Using picture as guide, pull each
drop into correct shape and block
if required.

Decorating the headband
Using picture as guide, place each
of the drops at a slight angle on the
headband one at a time, glue into
position and leave to dry before
adding the next drop.

Floral Hair Grips

Pretty flowers turn plain hair grips into a fun hair accessory for girls of all ages.
Use scraps of yarn to make a bouquet of them so that you have one to match every outfit.

YOU WILL NEED

Scraps of sport-weight cotton yarn in colours of choice
Pearl beads
Hair grips
Hot-glue gun
Size 2.75 mm (US C-2) hook

Tension

Tension is not important in this project

Dimensions

A flower measures approx 4 cm (1¾ in.) diameter

To make a flower

Using colour of choice, ch2.

Round 1: 10dc into 2nd ch from hook, sl st into first of ch2 at beg of round.

Round 2: ch2, 1tr into first 2sts, ch2, sl st into same st as last tr worked, *ch2, 1tr into next 2sts, ch2, sl st into same st as last tr worked, rep from * to end. (5 petals)

Round 3: working behind Round 2, sl st into stitch between petals (hook 2 loops to create a stable base to work from), *ch4, sl st in stitch between next petal, rep from * 4 times, ch4 sl st into first sl st to close. (5 ch4loops)

Round 4: sl st into first ch4sp, ch2, work [4tr, ch2] into same ch4sp, *ch2, work [4tr, ch2] into next ch4sp, rep from * to end. (5 petals)
Fasten off yarn and weave in loose ends.

Finishing

Glue pearl bead to centre of flower and leave to dry. Glue hair grip to back of crochet flower. Leave to dry.

Rainbow Wrist Cuffs

Make these gloves and your hands will thank you – they're
colourful, warm and stylish too.

YOU WILL NEED

Scraps of sport-weight wool blend yarn in
the following colours

MC	aqua
CCa	red
CCb	pink
CCc	light blue
CCd	teal
CCe	gold
CCf	lilac
CCg	medium blue
CCh	light green

14 buttons, 6mm (¼ in.) diameter
Size 3.5 mm (US E-4) hook

Tension
20 stitches by 11 rows over 10 cm (4 in.)
square using tr

Dimensions
Pattern is written to fit woman's medium-
sized hand.
To make larger, add a multiple of 3 to the
chain at the beginning of the pattern.
To make smaller, reduce by a multiple of 3
at the beginning of the pattern.

To make the left mitt

Using CCa, ch38.
Row 1: 1htr into 3rd ch from
hook, 1htr into each ch to end,
turn. (36sts)
Fasten off CCa and join in CCb.
Row 2: ch3, 1tr into each st to
end, turn.
Work the next 13 rows as Row 2,
changing colour for each row to
create stripe as follows.
Row 3: CCc.
Row 4: CCd.
Row 5: CCe.
Row 6: CCf.
Row 7: CCg.
Row 8: CCb.
Row 9: MC.
Row 10: CCh.
Row 11: CCa.
Row 12: CCd.
Row 13: CCc.
Row 14: CCe.
Row 15: CCb.

Work the next section of the mitt
as rounds.
Fasten off CCb and join in CCf.
Round 16: ch3, 1tr into each st
to end, sl st into top of ch3 at beg
of round.
Work the next two rounds as Round
16, changing colour for each round
to create stripe as follows.
Round 17: CCg.
Round 18: CCh.
Fasten off CCh and join in CCa.
Round 19: ch2, 1htr into each st
to end, sl st into top of ch2 at beg
of round.
Fasten off CCa and join in MC.

TOP EDGING
Round 20: ch1, 1dc into each st to
end, sl st into ch1 at beg of round.
Do not fasten off yarn.
Work next round working sl sts into
back loops only.

Round 21: *ch3, sl st into same st (picot made), sl st into next 3sts, rep from * to end.
Fasten off yarn.

Button Band

Lay mitt out so the rounds are on the left-hand side and the fold is to the bottom.
With RS facing you, join MC to the top right-hand corner and work button band as follows.
Row 1: ch3 (counts as first st), work 2tr into each stripe until 23sts have been worked.
Fasten off yarn.

Buttonhole Band

With RS facing you and using MC, work buttonhole band on opposite side from button band just worked. Join yarn to twelfth stripe from the left.
Row 1: ch1, 1dc into same sp, 2dc into each stripe to end, turn. (23sts)
Row 2: ch1, 1dc into first st, 1dc into next st, *ch2, miss 1st, 1dc into each of next 2sts, rep from * to end, turn. (7 buttonholes)
Row 3: miss 1st, sl st into next st, *3dc into ch2sp, sl st into next 2sts, rep from * 5 more times, 3dc into ch2sp, miss 1st, sl st into last st in row.

Fasten off yarn and weave in loose ends.

Thumb Hole

With RS facing, start work where the button band finished, into the thirteenth stripe.
Join MC into thirteenth stripe.
Round 1: ch1, 2dc into same place as ch1 just worked, continue working 2dc into each stripe up to where the rounds begin, next work back down the stripes until you have 16sts, miss the buttonhole band sts, working the first st firmly, work 2dc into the end of button band, sl st into first dc at beg of round. (18sts)
Round 2: ch1, 1dc into each st to end, sl st into ch1 at beg of round.
Fasten off yarn.

To make the right mitt

Work as given for left mitt until all 21 rows/rounds of mitt and top edging have been completed.

Buttonhole Band

Lay mitt out so the rounds are on the left-hand side and the fold is to the bottom.
Join MC to top right-hand corner and work buttonhole band as given for left mitt.

Button Band

With RS facing you, join MC to twelfth stripe from left and work button band on opposite side from buttonhole band as given for left mitt.

Thumb Hole

Work to match left mitt.

Finishing

Weave in loose ends and sew buttons onto button bands to match up with buttonholes.

Use scraps of yarn to make these colourful, striped wrist cuffs and dig into your jar of buttons to add a mismatched row of buttons.

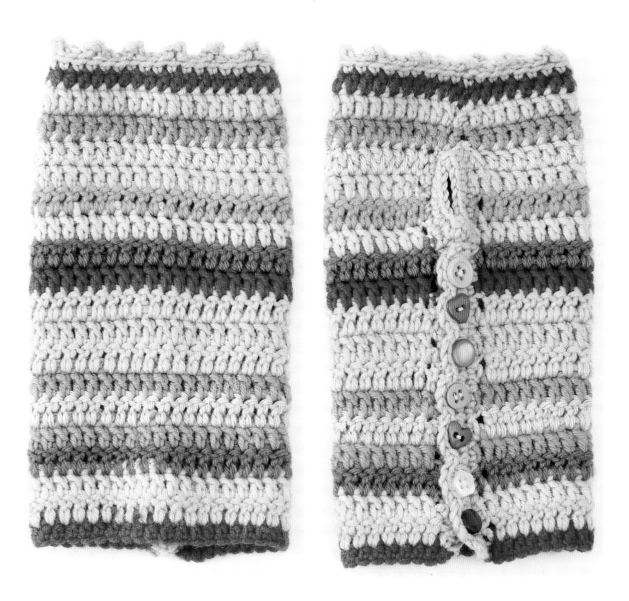

Slouch Hat

This cosy hat is perfect for crisp autumn days. The popcorn stitch adds texture and helps to showcase the soft, hand-dyed yarn.

YOU WILL NEED

Bulky-weight baby alpaca yarn (approx 100 g/3.5 oz; 100 m/109 yds.)
MC 1 ball in variegated orange/pink/orchid
Size 6 mm (US J-10) hook

Tension
4 popcorns to 10 cm (4 in.)

Dimensions
To fit a head 56 cm (22 in.) circumference

Special stitches
Popcorn stitch (tr4pop): work tr4 into the same stitch, drop loop from hook, insert hook from front to back through the top of the first tr and back into dropped loop, then pull it through the st to close
Popcorn stitch (tr3pop): work tr3 into the same stitch, drop loop from hook, insert hook from front to back through the top of the first tr and back into dropped loop, then pull it through the st to close

To make the hat

Using MC, make magic loop.

Round 1: ch3 (counts as first tr), work 11tr into ring, join with sl st into top of ch3 at beg of round. (12sts)

Round 2: ch3 (counts as first tr), 1tr into same place as base of ch3 just worked, 2tr into each st to end, sl st into ch3 at beg of round. (24sts)

Round 3: ch3 (counts as first tr), *2tr into next st, 1tr into next st, rep from * to last st, 2tr into last st, sl st into top of ch3 at beg of round.

Round 4: ch3 (counts as first tr), work tr3pop into base of ch3, ch2, miss 1st, *tr4pop into next st, ch2, miss 1st, rep from * to end, sl st into top of first popcorn. (18 popcorns)

Round 5: sl st into first ch2sp, ch3 (counts as first tr), 3tr into same ch2sp, *miss popcorn, 4tr into next ch2sp, rep from * to end, sl st into top of ch3 at beg of round. (72sts)

Round 6: ch3 (counts as first tr), 1tr into next 2sts, 2tr into next st, *1tr into next 3sts, 2tr into next st, rep from * to end, sl st into top of ch3 at beg of round. (90sts)

Round 7: ch3 (counts as first tr), work tr3pop into base of ch3, ch2, *miss 2sts, tr4pop into next st, rep from * to end, sl st into top of first popcorn. (30 popcorns)

Round 8: sl st into first ch2sp, ch3 (counts as first tr), 1tr into same ch2sp, *miss popcorn, 2tr into next ch2sp, rep from * to end, sl st into top of ch3 at beg of round. (60sts)

Round 9: ch3 (counts as first tr), 1tr into each st to end.

Round 10: as Round 7. (20 popcorns)

Round 11: sl st into first ch2sp, ch3 (counts as first tr), 2tr into same ch2sp, *miss popcorn, 3tr into next ch2sp, rep from * to end, sl st into top of ch3 at beg of round. (60sts)

Round 12: as Round 9.
Round 13: as Round 7.
(20 popcorns)
Round 14: as Round 8. (40sts)
Round 15: as Round 9.
Round 16: ch1 (counts as first dc),
2dc into next st, *1dc into next st,
2dc into next st, rep from * to end,
sl st into ch1 at beg of round. (60sts)
Round 17: ch1 (counts as first dc),
1dc into each st to end, sl st into ch1
at beg of round.
Repeat Round 17 twice more.

Finishing
Fasten off yarn and weave in
loose ends.

*Soft alpaca yarn
makes this hat
a pleasure to wear
- and it will garner
compliments
whenever
you wear it.*

Dancing Hearts Wrap

SKILL LEVEL

Perfect for cool summer evenings and early autumn mornings,
this heart-shaped wrap will keep the chill away.

YOU WILL NEED

Sport-weight acrylic yarn
(approx 100 g/3.5 oz; 311 m/350 yds.)

MC	1 ball in white
CCa	1 ball in light green
CCb	1 ball in medium green
CCc	1 ball in dark pink
CCd	1 ball in light pink

Size 6 mm (US J-10) hook

Tension
Tension is not important for this project but you will find it easier to use a hook one size larger than required by the yarn

Dimensions
150 x 80 cm (60 x 32 in.)
From edge to edge this heart-shaped wrap is 150 cm (60 in.) long. The heart shape is 80 cm (32 in.) deep.

Special stitches
Popcorn stitch (dtr3pop): work 3dtr in indicated st, drop loop from hook, insert hook from front to back through the top of the first dtr of the group, use hook to pull the dropped loop through the st to close. The first popcorn stitch of the round is worked with a ch4 as the first double treble.

To make the wrap
Using CCa, make magic loop.
Round 1: ch4 (counts as first dtr), dtr2pop into loop (first popcorn made), ch2, *dtr3pop into loop, ch2, rep from * 10 more times, sl st into top of first popcorn. (12 popcorns) Pull loop tight to close.
Round 2: ch7 (counts as 1dtr and ch3), *1dtr into next ch2sp, ch3, rep from * 10 more times, sl st into fourth of ch7 at beg of round. (12 ch3sp) Fasten off MC and join in CCc into any ch3sp.

Round 3: ch2 (counts as first st), work [2htr, 1tr, ch1, 1tr, 3htr] into same ch3sp, *miss next st, work [3htr, 1tr, ch1, 1tr, 3htr] into next ch3sp, rep from * 10 more times, sl st into top of ch2 at beg of round.
Round 4: ch1 (counts as first st), *miss next 3sts, work [4tr, ch2, 4tr] into next ch1sp, miss next 3sts**, 1dc in between next 2sts, rep from * 11 more times, ending last rep at **, sl st into ch1 at beg of round.
Fasten off and weave in loose ends.
Make a further 15 motifs as above, finishing after Round 4, and a further 18 motifs using CCb for Rounds 1–2 and CCd for Rounds 3–4.

Assembling the heart shape
Lay the motifs out in a heart shape before joining them. Lay 9 motifs in a shallow V shape (this will be the bottom edge). Alternate colours between light and dark motifs, so the edge motifs and centre motif

are light pink. Place a dark motif directly above the centre motif, and lay another 4 motifs each side, alternating colour. Place a light motif above the second-row centre motif, and lay another 4 motifs each side, alternating colour. For the final V, place the centre motif above the centre motif of the previous row and place 3 motifs each side to complete the heart shape.

Finishing
For each new motif, join MC to any dc on Round 4.
Round 5 (first motif): 1dc into same st, *ch4, miss 4 sts, work into next ch2sp [1dc, ch1, 1dc], ch4, miss 4 sts **, 1dc into next dc, rep from *, ending last rep at **, sl st into 1dc at beg of round.
Fasten off.

The repeated flower motifs are joined together using double crochet and slip stitches, which complement the lacy texture of the shawl.

Round 5 (each remaining motif): 1dc into same st, *ch4, miss 4 sts, work into next ch2sp either a joining edging-point [1dc, ch1, join with sl st into ch1sp of edged motif, 1dc] or a free edging-point [1dc, ch1, 1dc], ch4, miss 4 sts**, 1dc into next dc, rep from *, ending last rep at **, joining each motif into two of the ch2sp of the adjoining motif before joining into two of the ch2sp of the next adjacent edged motif (if there is one), to end the round, sl st into 1dc at beg of round.
Fasten off.
Weave in loose ends. Block wrap if required.

Wildflowers Scarf

Wrap yourself in a colourful garland of wildflowers. Wear the design long and skinny, layered like a cowl, or around your waist as a decorative belt.

YOU WILL NEED

Scraps of DK-weight cotton or wool yarn in assorted colours
Size 4 mm (US G-6) hook

Tension
Tension is not important in this project

Dimensions
A flower measures approx 11.5 cm (4½ in.) wide

To make the scarf

FIRST FLOWER MOTIF

Using colour of choice, ch6, join ends tog with sl st to form ring.
Round 1: ch3 (counts as first tr), 23tr into ring, sl st into top of ch3 at beg of round. (24sts)
Fasten off yarn and join colour of choice into any st.
Round 2: ch6 (counts as 1dc and ch5), *miss 1st, 1dc, ch3, miss 1st, 1dc, ch5, rep from * 4 more times, miss 1st, 1dc, ch3, sl st into first of ch6 at beg of round. (12 spaces)
Round 3: ch3 (counts as first tr), work [3tr, ch3, 4tr] into ch5sp, *1dc into next ch3sp, work [4tr, ch3, 4tr] into next ch5sp, rep from * 4 more times, 1dc into last ch3sp, sl st into top of ch3 at beg of round. (6 petals)
Fasten off yarn and weave in loose ends.

SECOND FLOWER MOTIF

Work Rounds 1–2 as given for first flower using colours of choice.
Join flowers together on Round 3 by working a sl st into matching ch3sp of top two petals, making sure the WS are together when joining as follows.
Round 3: ch3 (counts as first tr), work [3tr, ch1, sl st into corresponding ch3sp of first flower, ch1, 4tr] into first ch5sp, 1dc into next ch3sp, work [4tr, sl st into corresponding ch3sp of first flower, ch1, 4tr] into next ch5sp, *1dc into next ch3sp, work [4tr, ch3, 4tr] into next ch5sp, rep from * 3 more times, 1dc into last ch3sp, sl st into top of ch3 at beg of round.
Keep working motifs as given for second flower until scarf reaches desired length.

Finishing
Weave in loose ends and block if required.

Ombré String Cowl

SKILL LEVEL

This unusual cowl is perfect for crisp early autumn mornings – it adds just the right layer of warmth while you wait for the sun to work its magic.

YOU WILL NEED

Scraps of worsted-weight acrylic yarn
MC   berry
CCa   magenta
CCb   dark rose
CCc   light rose
CCd   pink
Size 5.5 mm (US I-9) hook

Tension
Tension is not important in this project

Dimensions
18 cm (7 in.) wide and 64 cm (25 in.) circumference

Special stitches
Back loop only (blo): The back loop of a chain refers to the back loop of the 'V' on the front of the chain. Put your hook through this loop when stitching into the ch.

To make the cowl
Using MC, ch90, join ends with sl st to form ring.

Round 1: ch1, 1dc into blo of each ch to end, join with sl st into ch1 at beg of round. (90sts)
Fasten off MC and join in CCa.

Round 2: sl st into blo of each st to end, sl st into first sl st at beg of round.

Round 3: ch1, 1dc into blo of same place as join, ch29, miss next 29sts, *1dc into next st on Round 1, ch29, miss next 29sts, rep from * once more, join with sl st into ch1 at beg of round.

Round 4: ch1, 1dc into blo of each st and ch to end, sl st into ch1 at beg of round.
Break off yarn and join in CCb.
The last three rounds form pattern; repeat Rounds 2–4 as follows.
Rounds 5–7: CCb.
Rounds 8–10: CCc.
Rounds 11–13: CCd.
Rounds 14–16: CCc.
Rounds 17–19: CCb.
Rounds 20–22: CCa.
Rounds 23–25: MC.
Round 26: as Round 2.

Finishing
Fasten off yarn and weave in loose ends.

Blossom Necklace

Adorn yourself with a necklace of colourful flowers. This delightful lariat-style necklace wraps and drapes daintily so why not crochet in all your favourite colours, from bold brights to soft pastels.

YOU WILL NEED

Scraps of sock, fingering, or sport-weight yarn – any smooth yarn with good stitch definition will work well in this project. You could also experiment with novelty yarns
Size 3.25 mm (US D-3) hook

Tension

Tension is not important in this project

Dimensions

A flower measures approx 4 x 4 cm (1½ x 1½ in.)

To make the scarf

FLOWER CENTRE

Using your colour of choice, make magic loop.
Round 1: ch2 (counts as first htr), work 17htr into ring, sl st into top of ch2 at beg of round. (18htr)
Fasten off yarn.

PETALS

Using colour of choice, join into any stitch of the flower centre with a sl st.
Round 1: ch3 (counts as first tr), 3tr into the same st, 1dc into next 2sts, *4tr into next st, 1dc into next 2sts, rep from * to end, sl st into top of ch3 at beg of round.
Fasten off yarn.
Make as many flowers as you wish in the colours of your choice.

STEM

With WS of flower facing, sl st into back loop of any of the dc petal stitches, ch4, miss htr, and sl st into base of stitch straight across from first sl st, ch10, then attach next flower in exactly the same way. Continue joining the flowers together until they have all been attached or the flower chain is the required length. Once you have attached the final flower work a further ch3.

Finishing

Fasten off yarn. Weave in loose ends.

Granny-Square Clutch Bag

SKILL LEVEL

Join pretty granny squares to make a clutch bag big enough to hold everything you need for a night out. Alternatively, brighten your desk using this colourful bag as a pencil case.

YOU WILL NEED

Sport-weight cotton yarn
(approx 50 g/1.76 oz; 121 m/132 yds.)
MC   1 ball in white
Scraps of yarn in 8 assorted colours
4 buttons, 18 mm (¾ in.) diameter
Size 2.75 mm (US C-2) hook

Tension
A square measures 5 cm (2 in.) square

Dimensions
10.5 x 20 cm (4¼ x 7¾ in.)

To make the clutch bag

GRANNY SQUARE (MAKE 16)
Using colour of choice, ch4 (counts as ch1 and 1tr).
Round 1: 1tr into 4th ch from hook, ch1, *2tr into same ch as first st, ch1, rep from * 5 more times, sl st into top of initial ch4. (8 petals)
Sl st into first tr of Round 1 and break off yarn. Join colour of choice into first ch1sp.
Round 2: ch3 (counts as first tr), 2tr into same ch1sp, *miss next 2sts, work [3tr, ch2, 3tr] into next ch1sp**, miss 2sts, 3tr into next ch1sp, rep from * 3 more times, ending last rep at **, sl st into top of ch3 at beg of round.
Fasten off yarn and join MC into first tr of 3tr on any side.
Round 3: ch1, 1dc into next 5sts, *work [1dc, ch1, 1dc] into next ch2sp, 1dc into next 9sts, rep from * twice more, work [1dc, ch1, 1dc] into last ch2sp, 1dc into last 3sts, sl st into ch1 at beg of round.
Weave in loose ends.

Finishing

Sew the squares together as follows.
Place first two squares with RS together, then using MC, work whip stitch through the back loops only. Repeat this process until you have two sets of 2 x 4 squares.
With RS facing you and using MC, join yarn to first st just after the corner.
Round 1: ch1, *1dc into each st to corner, work [1dc, ch1, 1dc] into corner (corner made), rep from * to end, sl st into ch1 at beg of round.
Repeat Round 1 once more.
Fasten off yarn.
Place panels with RS together, then sew together using same method as squares. Work around three edges only, leaving top open.
Weave in loose ends and turn clutch RS out.

Using picture as guide, attach a button to the centre top of each square just below the opening.
Turn clutch over so the opposite side from the button panel is facing.
Using MC, join yarn to centre top of square, making sure you match position of each button, ch6, miss 1st and sl st into next st.
Fasten off yarn and weave in loose ends.
Repeat this for remaining buttons.

Mobile Phone and Tablet Covers

Use up all your odds and ends of yarn and give your phone and tablet
a unique and colourful protective cover.

YOU WILL NEED

Scraps of DK-weight acrylic/nylon blend yarn

CCa	1 ball in yellow
CCb	1 ball in light green
CCc	1 ball in red
CCd	1 ball in purple
CCe	1 ball in orange
CCf	1 ball in pink
CCg	1 ball in blue

3 buttons 18 mm (¾ in.) diameter for phone cover

4 buttons 32 mm (1½ in.) diameter for tablet cover

Size 4 mm (US G-6) hook

Size 5 mm (US H-8) hook

Tension
Not important but check to make sure panel will fit mobile phone or tablet snugly

Dimensions
Mobile phone cover: 15 x 9 cm (6 x 3½ in.)
Tablet cover: 24 x 17.5 cm (9½ x 7 in.)

To make the mobile phone cover

PANEL (MAKE 2)

Using 5 mm hook and CCa, ch23.
Change to 4 mm hook.

Row 1: 1dc into 2nd ch from hook, 1dc into each ch to end, turn. (22sts)

Row 2: ch1 (counts as first st), 1dc into each st and tch to end. (22sts)

Fasten off CCa and join in CCb.

Work each row as Row 2 in the following stripe sequence:

Rows 3 and 4: CCb.

Rows 5 and 6: CCc.

Rows 7 and 8: CCd.

Rows 9 and 10: CCe.

Rows 11 and 12: CCf.

Fasten off yarn. Weave in loose ends. Block front and back panels to correct size.

Finishing

With WS together, join front and back panels as follows using yarn CCg and 4 mm hook.

Insert hook at the top right-hand corner of both front and back panels, yoh and draw through, work sl st to secure, ch1, 1dc into same place as you joined the yarn, *work 1dc into each stitch, matching up the front and back panels until you reach first corner, work 3dc into corner (first corner made), rep from * until second corner made, then continue working back up to the top opening. Do not fasten off yarn.

Work top opening in rounds as follows.

Round 1: ch1, work 1dc into each stitch around the opening, sl st into ch1 at beg of round.

Fasten off CCg and join in CCc.

Next round: ch1, 1dc into each st from joining of the panels, working 3dc into each corner, then work as Round 1 of top opening.

Fasten off yarn and weave in loose ends.

To make the tablet cover

PANEL (MAKE 2)

Using 5 mm hook and CCa, ch38.
Change to 4 mm hook.
Row 1: 1dc into 2nd ch from hook,
1dc into each ch to end, turn.
(38sts)
Row 2: ch1 (counts as first dc), 1dc
into each st and tch to end, turn.
The last row forms pattern; repeat
Row 2 twice more.
Work each row as Row 2 in the
following stripe sequence:
Rows 5–8: CCb.
Rows 9–12: CCc.
Rows 13–16: CCd.
Rows 17–20: CCe.
Rows 21–24: CCf.
Rows 25–28: CCg.
Rows 29–32: CCa.
Rows 33–36: CCb.
Fasten off yarn and weave in
loose ends.
Block front and back panels to
correct size.

Finishing

With WS together, join front and
back panels together as follows using
CCc and 4 mm hook.
Insert hook at the top right-hand
corner of both front and back panels,
yoh and draw through, work sl st to
secure, ch1, 1dc into same place as

you joined the yarn, *work 1dc into
each stitch, matching up the front
and back panels, until you reach first
corner, work 3dc into corner (first
corner made), repeat from * until
second corner made, then continue
working back up to the top opening.
Do not fasten off yarn.
Work top opening in rounds
as follows.
Round 1: ch1, work 1dc into each
stitch around the opening, sl st into
ch1 at beg of round.
Fasten off CCc and join in CCd.
Round 2: as Round 1.
Round 2 forms repeat; repeat in the
following stripe sequence.
Round 3: CCe.
Round 4: CCf.
Round 5: CCg.
Fasten off yarn and weave in
loose ends.

To make the loop

Using 4 mm hook and CCb and
leaving long tail, ch24, join ends
with sl st form loop.
Round 1: ch1, 24dc into loop,
sl st into ch1 at beg of round.
Fasten off yarn, leaving long tail.
Pin loop to inside centre back of
case just below the start of the
top opening.

Stitch into position using long tails.
Sew button to centre front panel to
match loop, then add three more
buttons for decoration if desired.

This design features vertical stripes rather than the usual horizontal ones. Summery seaside colours add to the fun.

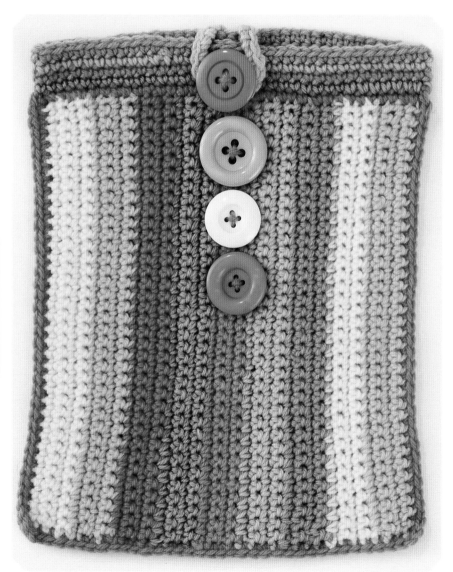

Star Backpack

Youngsters – and the young at heart – will enjoy filling this spacious bag with their belongings. Keep an eye on your work so that the stitches are close together and there are no gaps in the fabric.

YOU WILL NEED

Scraps of sport-weight cotton yarn in 14 assorted colours
Size 2.75 mm (US C-2) hook for bag and stars
Size 4 mm (US G-6) hook for bag ties
Sitch marker
Polyester toy filling for stuffing stars

Tension
Tension is not important in this project

Dimensions
42 cm (16½ in.) high

To make the bag

BASE (MAKE 1)

Using 2.75 mm hook and colour of choice, ch4, join ends with sl st to form ring.

Round 1: ch3 (counts as first tr), 10tr into ring, sl st into top of ch3 at beg of round. (11sts)

Round 2: ch3 (counts as first tr), 1tr into same st, 2tr into each st to end, sl st into top of ch3 at beg of round. (22sts)

Round 3: ch3 (counts as first tr), 1tr into same st, 1tr into next st, *2tr into next st, 1tr into next st, rep from * to end, sl st into top of ch3 at beg of round. (33sts)

Round 4: ch3 (counts as first tr), 1tr into same st, 1tr into next 2sts, *2tr into next st, 1tr into next 2sts, rep from * to end, sl st into top of ch3 at beg of round. (44sts)

Round 5: ch3 (counts as first tr), 1tr into same st, 1tr into next 3sts, *2tr into next st, tr1 into next 3sts, rep from * to end, sl st into top of ch3 at beg of round. (55sts)

Round 6: ch3 (counts as first tr), 1tr into same st, 1tr into next 4sts, *2tr into next st, 1tr into next 4sts, rep from * to end, sl st into top of ch3 at beg of round. (66sts)

Fasten off yarn and join in colour of choice.

Keep working as set, adding 1st every round in between increases until 231sts.

To make the bag smaller, stop increasing when the finished number of stitches is divisible by 3.

To make the bag bigger, continue increasing as set, finishing when the number of stitches is divisible by 3.

BODY (MAKE 1)

Make body of bag as follows, changing colours at the end of each round to create the stripe pattern.

Round 1: ch4 (counts as 1tr and ch1), 1tr into same st, *miss 2sts, work [1tr, ch1, 1tr] into next st, rep from * to end, sl st into 3rd ch of ch4 at beg of round.

Sl st into ch1sp, fasten off yarn and join in colour of choice.

Round 2: ch4 (counts as 1tr and ch1), 1tr into ch1sp, *miss 2sts, work [1tr, ch1, 1tr] into next ch1sp, rep from * to end, sl st into 3rd ch of ch4 at beg of round.

Repeat Round 2 until 28 rounds have been worked or the bag is required length.

Fasten off yarn and weave in loose ends.

TOP FLAP

Using 2.75 mm hook and colour of choice, ch42.

Row 1: 1tr into 4th ch from hook, 1tr into each ch to end, turn. (39sts + 1tch)

Row 2: ch3 (counts as first tr), 1tr into each st and tch, turn. (40sts)
Fasten off yarn and join in colour of choice.
Repeat Row 2 until nine rows have been worked, changing colour every two rows to form stripe.
Row 10: ch3 (count as first tr), tr2tog over next 2sts, 1tr into each st until 1st remains, miss the last st, turn. (38sts)
Repeat Row 10 until 22sts, keeping stripe correct.
Fasten off yarn and join in colour of choice.
Work edging around top flap as follows.
Round 1: ch1, 2dc around each st up to top, 1dc along straight edge, 2dc around each st down the side to bottom section, 1dc along to beg of round, sl st into ch1 at beg of round.
Fasten off yarn and join in colour of choice.
Round 2: as Round 1.
Fasten off yarn.
Attach top flap to bag, pinning into position and then sew into place.

Bag handles (make 2)

Using 2.75 mm hook and colour of choice, ch13.
Row 1: 1tr into 4th ch from hook, 1tr into each ch to end, turn. (11sts)

Row 2: ch3, 1tr into each st to end, turn.
Repeat last row until approx 102 rows have been worked or until handle is required length.
Pin and stitch both handles into position at top and bottom of the bag.
Weave in loose ends.

Bag ties

Using 4 mm hook and six strands of yarn held together, work chain until required length.
Fasten off yarn.
Weave chain through top row of Vs of bag.

Stars (make 2)

This design is worked in a spiral. Do not close rounds with a sl st; place a marker to help you identify where the end of the round is.
Using 2.75 mm hook and colour of choice, ch2.
Round 1: 5dc into 2nd ch from hook. (5sts)
Round 2: 2dc into each st to end. (10sts)
Round 3: *1dc into next st, 2dc into next st, rep from * to end. (15sts)
Round 4: *1dc into next 2sts, 2dc into next st, rep from * to end. (20sts)

Work star points as follows in rows.
Row 1: 1dc into next 4sts, turn. (4sts)
Row 2: ch1, 1dc into each st to end, turn. (4sts)
Row 3: ch1, miss next st, 1dc into each st to end, turn. (3sts)
Repeat Row 3.
Fasten off yarn.
Rejoin yarn to next st after the base of first point on main spiral section and repeat rows.
On the last point, do not fasten off yarn. Work edge as follows.
Work *4dc down point, sl st in between points, 4dc up next point, 1dc into top of point, rep from * until all five points have been worked.
Fasten off yarn and weave in loose ends. Block if required.

Finishing

Place stars with WS together and sew around the outer edge, inserting stuffing as you go. Use a pencil or similar to make sure the stuffing fills the point.
Sew star to the bag ties.
Repeat pattern for second star using a different colour.

The Weekender Bag

Destined to become your favourite bag, this tote is lots of fun to make and perfect
for weekend adventures – or for holding your yarn stash.

Large bag

YOU WILL NEED

Worsted-weight acrylic yarn (approx
100 g/3.5 oz; 156 m/170 yds.)
MC   2 balls in white
CCa   1 ball in rust
CCb   1 ball in terra cotta
58 cm (23 in.) zip for large bag
2 metal circle rings, 3.75 mm (1½ in.)
diameter, for attaching handle
112 cm (44 in.) long strap with latch hooks
on each end
Size 3.75 mm (US F-5) hook for base
Size 4 mm (US G-6) hook for bag

Tension

Using 3.75 mm hook, approx 20 stitches
by 18 rows over 10 cm (4 in.) square
using pattern
Using 4 mm hook, approx 16 stitches by 16
rows over 10 cm (4 in.) square using pattern

Dimensions

Approx 15 x 40 cm (6 x 16 in.) at bottom,
38 cm (15 in.) tall, 58.5 cm (23 in.) across
the top

Small bag

YOU WILL NEED

Worsted-weight acrylic yarn (approx
100 g/3.5 oz; 156 m/170 yds.)
MC   2 balls in white
CCa   1 ball in honey
CCb   1 ball in mustard
46 cm (18 in.) zip for small bag
2 metal circle rings, 3.75 mm (1½ in.)
diameter, for attaching handle
112 cm (44 in.) long strap with latch hooks
on each end
Size 3.75 mm (US F-5) hook for base
Size 4 mm (US G-6) hook for bag

Tension

Using 3.75 mm hook, approx 20 stitches
by 18 rows over 10 cm (4 in.) square
using pattern
Using 4 mm hook, approx 16 stitches by 16
rows over 10 cm (4 in.) square using pattern

Dimensions

Approx 9 x 30 cm (3½ x 12 in.) at bottom,
31 cm (12½ in.) tall, 43 cm (17 in.) across
the top

To make the bag

When working with colour changing,
the colour not being used is worked
through the centre of the stitch. For
solid row colours, the opposite colour
does not need to be worked through
the centre.

NOTE: Instructions are given for the
small size first, large size in ( ).

BASE (MAKE 1)

Using 3.75 mm hook and MC,
ch55(67).
Row 1: 1dc into 2nd ch from hook,
1dc into each st to end, turn.
(54 (66)sts)
Row 2: ch1, 1dc into each st to
end, turn.
Repeat Row 2 a further 16 (28) times
or until base is the correct width.
Do not fasten off yarn.

SIDES (MAKE 1)

Change to 4 mm hook and work the
sides of the bag in rounds.

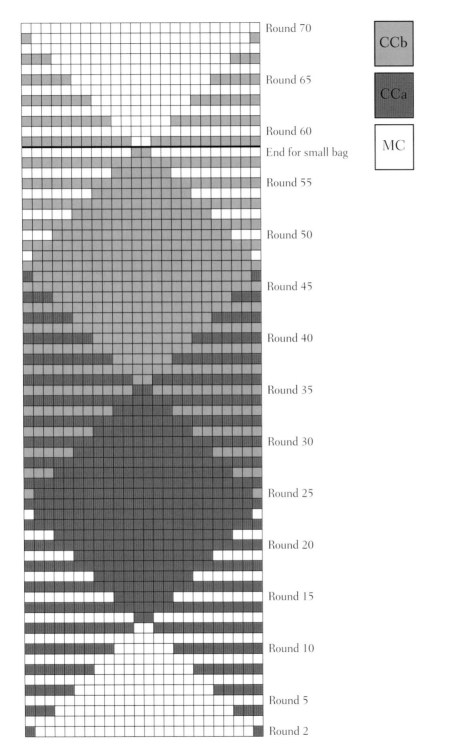

Round 70

CCb

Round 65

CCa

Round 60

End for small bag

MC

Round 55

Round 50

Round 45

Round 40

Round 35

Round 30

Round 25

Round 20

Round 15

Round 10

Round 5

Round 2

Round 1: using MC, ch1, 1dc into each st around the outer edge of the base, sl st into ch1 at beg of round. (144 (192)sts)

Do not fasten off MC; join in CCa. This colour pattern is worked in a series of 24st repeats. See chart (left) for visual reference.

Round 2: using CCa, ch1, *1dc into first st; using MC, 1dc into next 22sts; using CCa, 1dc into next st, rep from * to end, sl st into ch1 at beg of round.

Round 3: using MC, ch1, 1dc into each st to end, sl st into ch1 at beg of round.

Round 4: using CCa, ch1, *1dc into next 3sts; using MC, 1dc into next 18sts; using CCa, 1dc into next 3sts, rep from * to end, sl st into ch1 at beg of round.

Round 5: as Round 3.

Round 6: using CCa, ch1, *1dc into next 5sts; using MC, 1dc into next 14sts; using CCa, 1dc into next 5sts, rep from * to end, sl st into ch1 at beg of round.

Round 7: as Round 3.

Round 8: using CCa, ch1, *1dc into next 7sts; using MC, 1dc into next 10sts; using CCa, 1dc into next 7sts, rep from * to end, sl st into ch1 at beg of round.

Round 9: as Round 3.

Round 10: using CCa, ch1, *1dc

into next 9sts; using MC, 1dc into next 6sts; using CCa, 1dc into next 9sts, rep from * to end, sl st into ch1 at beg of round.

Round 11: as Round 3.

Round 12: using CCa, ch1, *1dc into next 11sts; using MC, 1dc into next 2sts; using CCa, 1dc into next 11sts, rep from * to end, sl st into ch1 at beg of round.

Round 13: using MC, ch1, *1dc into next 11sts; using CCa, 1dc into next 2sts; using MC, 1dc into next 11sts, rep from * to end, sl st into ch1 at beg of round.

Round 14: using CCa, ch1, 1dc into each st to end, sl st into ch1 at beg of round.

Round 15: using MC, ch1, *1dc into next 9sts; using CCa, 1dc into next 6sts; using MC, 1dc into next 9sts, rep from * to end, sl st into ch1 at beg of round.

Round 16: as Round 14.

Round 17: using MC, ch1, *1dc into next 7sts; using CCa, 1dc into next 10sts; using MC, 1dc into next 7sts, rep from * to end, sl st into ch1 at beg of round.

Round 18: as Round 14.

Round 19: using MC, ch1, *1dc into next 5sts; using CCa, 1dc into next 14sts; using MC, 1dc into next 5sts, rep from * to end, sl st into ch1 at beg of round.

Round 20: as Round 14.

Round 21: using MC, ch1, *1dc into next 3sts; using CCa, 1dc into next 18sts; using MC, 1dc into next 3sts, rep from * to end, sl st into ch1 at beg of round.

Round 22: as Round 14.

Round 23: using MC, ch1, *1dc into next st; using CCa, 1dc into next 22sts; using MC, 1dc into next st, rep from * to end, sl st into ch1 at beg of round.

Break off MC.

Round 24: as Round 14.

Do not break off CCa; join in CCb.

Round 25: using CCb, ch1, *1dc into next st; using CCa, 1dc into next 22sts; using CCb, 1dc into next st, rep from * to end, sl st into ch1 at beg of round.

Round 26: as Round 14.

Round 27: using CCb, ch1, *1dc into next 3sts; using CCa, 1dc into next 18sts; using CCb, 1dc into next 3sts, rep from * to end, sl st into ch1 at beg of round.

Round 28: as Round 14.

Round 29: using CCb, ch1, *1dc into next 5sts; using CCa, 1dc into next 14sts; using CCb, 1dc into next 5sts, rep from * to end, sl st into ch1 at beg of round.

Round 30: as Round 14.

Round 31: using CCb, ch1, *1dc into next 7sts; using CCa, 1dc into next 10sts; using CCb, 1dc into next 7sts, rep from * to end, sl st into ch1 at beg of round.

Round 32: as Round 14.

Round 33: using CCb, ch1, *1dc into next 9sts; using CCa, 1dc into next 6sts; using CCb, 1dc into next 9sts, rep from * to end, sl st into ch1 at beg of round.

Round 34: as Round 14.

Round 35: using CCb, ch1, *1dc into next 11sts; using CCa, 1dc into next 2sts; using CCb, 1dc into next 11sts, rep from * to end, sl st into ch1 at beg of round.

Round 36: using CCa, ch1, *1dc into next 11sts; using CCb, 1dc into next 2sts; using CCa, 1dc into next 11sts, rep from * to end, sl st into ch1 at beg of round.

Round 37: using CCb, ch1, 1dc into each st to end, sl st into ch1 at beg of round.

Round 38: using CCa, ch1, *1dc into next 9sts; using CCb, 1dc into next 6sts; using CCa, 1dc into next 9sts, rep from * to end, sl st into ch1 at beg of round.

Round 39: as Round 37.

Round 40: using CCa, ch1, *1dc into next 7sts; using CCb, 1dc into next 10sts; using CCa, 1dc into next 7sts, rep from * to end, sl st into ch1 at beg of round.

Round 41: as Round 37.

Round 42: using CCa, ch1, *1dc into next 5sts; using CCb, 1dc into next 14sts; using CCa, 1dc into next 5sts, rep from * to end, sl st into ch1 at beg of round.

Round 43: as Round 37.

Round 44: using CCa, ch1, *1dc into next 3sts; using CCb, 1dc into next 18sts; using CCa, 1dc into next 3sts, rep from * to end, sl st into ch1 at beg of round.

Round 45: as Round 37.

Round 46: using CCa, ch1, *1dc into next st; using CCb, 1dc into next 22sts; using CCa, 1dc into next st, rep from * to end, sl st into ch1 at beg of round.

Round 47: as Round 37.
Fasten off CCa and rejoin MC.

Round 48: using MC, ch1, *1dc into next st; using CCb, 1dc into next 22sts; using MC, 1dc into next st, rep from * to end, sl st into ch1 at beg of round.

Round 49: as Round 37.

Round 50: using MC, ch1, *1dc into next 3sts; using CCb, 1dc into next 18sts; using MC, 1dc into next 3sts, rep from * to end, sl st into ch1 at beg of round.

Round 51: as Round 37.

Round 52: using MC, ch1, *1dc into next 5sts; using CCb, 1dc into next 14sts; using MC, 1dc into next 5sts, rep from * to end, sl st into ch1 at beg of round.

Round 53: as Round 37.

Round 54: using MC, ch1, *1dc into next 7sts; using CCb, 1dc into next 10sts; using MC, 1dc into next 7sts, rep from * to end, sl st into ch1 at beg of round.

Round 55: as Round 37.

Round 56: using MC, ch1, *1dc into next 9sts; using CCb, 1dc into next 6sts; using MC, 1dc into next 9sts, rep from * to end, sl st into ch1 at beg of round.

Round 57: as Round 37.

Round 58: using MC, ch1, *1dc into next 11sts; using CCb, 1dc into next 2sts; using MC, 1dc into next 11sts, rep from * to end, sl st into ch1 at beg of round.

Small bag only

Round 59: Using MC, ch1, 1dc into each st to end, sl st into ch1 at beg of round. Fasten off yarn.

Large bag only

Round 59: using CCb, ch1, *1dc into next 11sts; using MC, 1dc into next 2sts; using CCb, 1dc into next 11sts, rep from * to end, sl st into ch1 at beg of round.
Round 60: as Round 3.
Round 61: using CCb, ch1, *1dc into next 9sts; using MC, 1dc into next 6sts; using CCb, 1dc into next 9sts, rep from * to end, sl st into ch1 at beg of round.
Round 62: as Round 3.
Round 63: using CCb, ch1, *1dc into next 7sts; using MC, 1dc into next 10sts; using CCb, 1dc into next 7sts, rep from * to end, sl st into ch1 at beg of round.
Round 64: as Round 3.
Round 65: using CCb, ch1, *1dc into next 5sts; using MC, 1dc into next 14sts; using CCb, 1dc into next 5sts, rep from * to end, sl st into ch1 at beg of round.
Round 66: as Round 3.
Round 67: using CCb, ch1, *1dc into next 3sts; using MC, 1dc into next 18sts; using CCb, 1dc into next 3sts, rep from * to end, sl st into ch1 at beg of round.

Round 68: as Round 3.
Round 69: using CCb, ch1, *1dc into next st; using MC, 1dc into next 22sts; using CCb, 1dc into next st, rep from * to end, sl st into ch1 at beg of round.
Round 70: as Round 3.
Fasten off yarn. Weave in loose ends.

Finishing

Using picture as guide, fold the top of the bag so the top corner of the bag is even with the centre of each end of the rectangle piece at the bottom.

Next, pin and then hand sew the zip to the top of the bag, then sew the remaining open parts of the bag on each end of the zip closed with your needle and thread.

Make loops for handle as follows.
Using 3.75 mm hook and CCb, ch9.
Row 1: 1dc into 2nd ch from hook, 1dc into each ch to end, turn. (8sts)
Row 2: ch1, 1dc into each st to end, turn.
Repeat Row 2 six more times.
Fasten off yarn and weave in loose ends.
Loop square just worked through metal ring, then sew onto side of bag approx 7.5 cm (3 in.) from top on large bag and 4 cm (1½ in.) on small bag (see above right). Repeat this for second loop.

Attach the strap. It can be latched onto each ring to make a long cross-body bag, or folded in half and looped through one side, both latches being hooked on the opposite side to make it an over-the-shoulder bag.

Crochet TECHNIQUES

Whether you want to learn the basics, or just need to refresh your memory about one or two stitches or other techniques, you'll find all the information you need to make the projects in this book in this chapter.

Tools and Materials

Choosing the yarn for a project is great fun. However, it's important to know a little bit about the basic properties of yarns, such as their weights and fibres, before you begin. As well as yarn you will, of course, need a crochet hook to crochet with, but there are one or two other pieces of equipment you will find useful. The information below gives a brief introduction to some of the items you will need to have in your work box.

Yarns

There are three types of yarn fibre: animal, plant and synthetic. Many yarns blend different fibres together to produce more durable yarns that can be machine washed and dried.

The most common animal fibre is sheep's wool. It is warm, insulating, absorbent and quite elastic, making it easy to crochet with. Other commonly used animal fibres are mohair, cashmere, angora, alpaca and silk.

Plant fibres, such as cotton, linen, hemp, soya and bamboo, are lightweight, breathe well and are ideal for warm-weather garments.

Synthetic (man-made) fibres include acrylic, nylon, polyester and rayon. Yarns made from them are durable, inexpensive and machine washable, making them perfect for items that need frequent washing.

Fibres are spun into yarns of different thicknesses referred to as 'weights.' The names of the different weights vary from country to country. Each one has a tension and recommended hook size; use these as a guideline when choosing yarn, but always check your tension (see page 115) as you want to match the tension of the pattern you are crocheting and knowing the weight of a yarn is important should you decide to substitute one yarn for another.

You should find all the information you need to know about a yarn on the label. Most should include the knitting tension, but not all will include the crochet tension. If so, use the knitting tension. Choose a hook one size larger than the recommended knitting needle size.

Always buy enough yarn in the same colour and dye lot to complete a particular project.

Tools

Crochet hooks are available in many styles – from basic aluminium, wood and plastic to ergonomic designs with molded-plastic handles. Try out a few to see which you prefer and remember that some hooks work better with different types of yarn. For example, a wooden hook will grip the yarn, making it ideal for slippery silks, while sleek aluminium hooks tend to work well with rougher woolen yarns.

The size of a modern hook will be marked on the handle – either the US letter/numbering system, or the metric size, or both. If you cannot find this, use a knitting tension – a piece of plastic or wood with holes drilled in it. Slide the shaft of the hook into the holes until you find the perfect fit.

A small pair of scissors with sharp blades are useful for cutting and trimming yarn ends. As well as measuring your crochet, a retractable tape measure is useful when checking your tension.

Sew in yarn ends and join sections using a blunt tapestry needle with an eye large enough to accommodate your yarn. Hold fabrics together for

sewing and in place when blocking, with the large glass-headed, rust-free pins used by quilters.

Some patterns require stitch markers to help you to keep track of the beginning of continuous rounds or pattern repeats and for counting stitches. These can be as simple as a scrap of yarn or a safety pin, but make sure they have open ends and can be removed easily without snagging your yarn.

Designs such as the Chevron Pillow (see page 38) and the Star Backpack (see page 100) require small amounts of different colours of yarn. You will find that these are easier to work with if they are wound onto bobbins, or around small pieces of cardboard, than if you try to work with larger balls of yarn.
You can also use the bobbins to store scraps of yarn neatly.

Experiment with different colourways to create vibrant variations unique to you.

Getting Started

Holding the hook and yarn

There are two ways to hold the hook: the knife hold and the pencil hold. Use the one you find most comfortable. To create tension on the yarn so that you can form stitches evenly, hold the working yarn in your non-dominant hand.

KNIFE HOLD

Hold the flat section or middle of the hook lightly between your thumb and forefinger.

WOVEN

Weave the yarn over your index finger, under the middle finger and over your ring finger. If this feels loose, wrap it around your little finger.

PENCIL HOLD

Use the tips of your thumb and forefinger to hold the hook lightly on the flat section or middle of the hook.

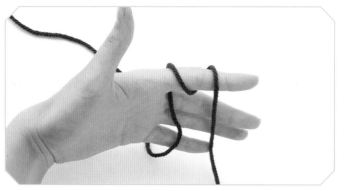

FOREFINGER

Wrap the yarn twice around your forefinger.

Tension

For many projects in this book, checking and maintaining your tension to ensure that your finished crochet is the correct size is not essential. However, it is necessary for some items and, for these, you should work a swatch before you start.

Each pattern will indicate the tension. For example: 10 cm (4 in.) = 15 double treble crochet (dtr) and 9 rows using size 5 mm hook. However, everyone's tension is different.

To check your tension, crochet a 15 cm (6 in.) square using the hook size, yarn and stitch pattern (in this example, double treble crochet) stated in the pattern. Place a ruler horizontally across a row of stitches in the centre of the square and insert pins at the 0 and 10 cm (4 in.) marks. Then count the stitches between the pins – including any partial stitches. For this example do you have 15 stitches? If you have too many, make a second square using a hook one size larger. If you have too few, use a hook one size smaller. Keep making squares until you have the correct tension. Check the vertical tension in the same way, counting the number of rows between the pins – including any partial rows – and adjust the hook size as necessary.

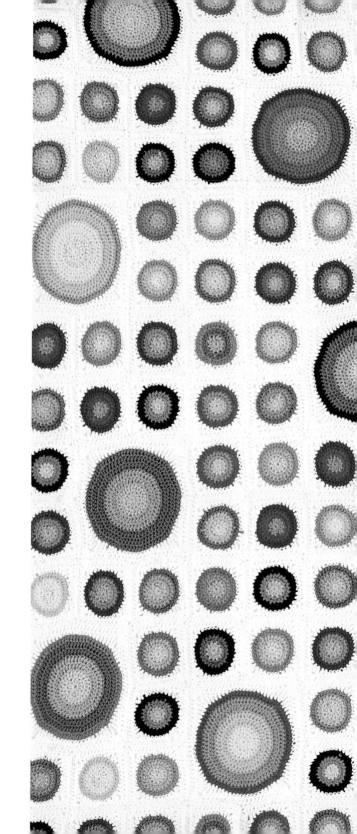

Making a slip knot

Wrap the yarn clockwise around your forefinger and cross it over the working yarn leaving a 15 cm (6 in.) tail (you will weave this in later). Insert the hook in front of the original loop but behind the tail end of the yarn. Slide the loop off your finger while pinching the X overlap you just made. Hold both yarn ends and pull them tight, but not too tight, around your hook.

Foundation chain and chain stitches

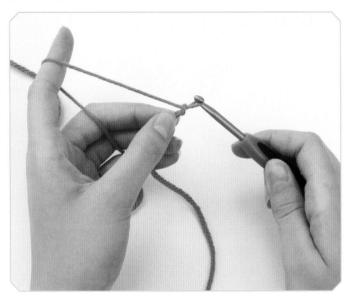

The foundation chain is a little like casting on when knitting – it's the starting point for working new stitches. As you work the chain, keep moving your fingers up the chain to hold the latest stitch. Make a slip knot on your hook and hold it with the thumb and middle finger of your yarn hand. Bring the working yarn from behind and over the hook (this is referred to as a 'yarn over the hook'). Use the hook to pull the yarn through the loop on your hook. You have made one chain stitch. Repeat to make the required number of chains, but remember that the loop on your hook never counts as a chain stitch.

Working into the chain

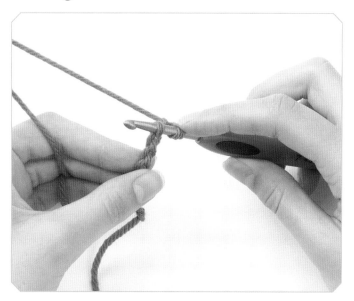

The first row of crochet stitches is worked into the chain. From the front each chain forms a V shape; from the back each one has a ridge that forms a spine. There are three ways to do this, each one giving a different result. Working through the top loop of the chain is the simplest method but may leave gaps between the stitches. Working through the back ridge only will give the first row the same look as the last, making it ideal if you are not giving your finished project a border or edging. Alternatively you can work through the top loop and back ridge at the same time.

Turning chains

Turning chains are essential to bring the first stitch of a row or round up to the proper height. This is why a pattern will tell you to miss chains before you work your first stitch into the foundation chain. A slip stitch does not require a turning chain. Double crochet has one chain but this is not counted as a stitch. Half treble crochet has two turning chains; these sometimes count as a stitch. Treble crochet requires three turning chains and these are counted as a stitch. Four chains are used with double treble crochet and these also count as a stitch.

Stitches

Double crochet (dc)

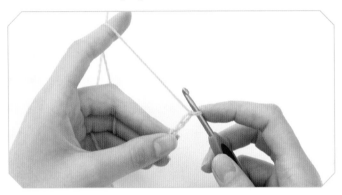

1 Insert the hook into the second chain from the hook.

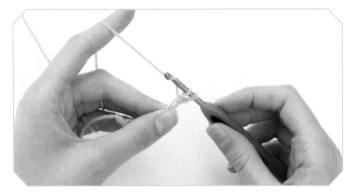

3 Yarn over the hook and pull it through both loops on the hook to complete the stitch. Insert the hook into the next chain and repeat Steps 2 and 3. Repeat this sequence into each chain.

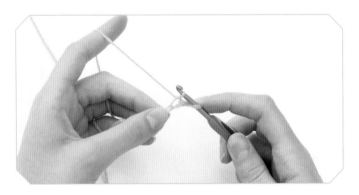

2 Yarn over the hook and pull up a loop to make two loops on the hook.

4 To work the next row, make one chain and turn the work. Insert the hook into the first stitch under the top two loops and complete Steps 2 and 3. Continue across the row. Do not work a stitch into the turning chain of the previous row.

Half treble crochet (htr)

1 Yarn over the hook and insert the hook into the third chain from the hook.

2 Yarn over the hook and pull up a loop to make three loops on the hook.

3 Yarn over the hook and draw through all three loops on the hook to complete the stitch. Yarn over the hook, insert the hook into the next chain and complete Steps 2 and 3. Repeat into each chain across.

4 To work the next row, make two chains and turn the work. Insert the hook into the second stitch (missing the first stitch because the two turning chains count as a stitch).

5 Work under the top two loops and complete Steps 2 and 3. Continue working stitches into each stitch across the row. Make the last stitch into the top chain of the previous row's turning chain.

Counting the two turning chains as a stitch can leave gaps in the row edges. As a result, some patterns do not count them as a stitch. If this is the case, work the first stitch of the row into the first stitch and do not work a stitch into the turning chain at the end of the row. Follow the pattern instructions closely and make sure the stitch count for each row or round matches the stitch count given in the pattern.

Treble crochet (tr)

1 Yarn over the hook and insert the hook into the fourth chain from the hook.

2 Yarn over the hook and pull up a loop. There will be three loops on the hook.

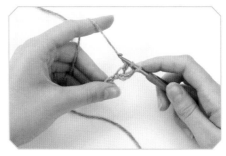

3 Yarn over the hook and draw through two loops. There will be two loops on the hook.

4 Yarn over the hook and draw through two loops to complete the stitch. Yarn over the hook, insert the hook into the next chain and complete Steps 2 to 4. Repeat into each chain across.

5 To work the next row, make three chains and turn the work. Insert the hook into the second stitch (missing the first stitch because the three turning chains count as a stitch). Work under the top two loops and complete Steps 2 to 4.

6 Continue working stitches into each stitch across the row. The last stitch will be made into the top chain of the previous row's turning chain.

Double treble crochet (dtr)

1 Yarn over the hook twice and insert the hook into the fifth chain from the hook.

3 Yarn over the hook and draw through two loops. There will be three loops on the hook.

5 Yarn over the hook and draw through two loops to complete the stitch. Yarn over the hook twice and insert the hook into the next chain and complete Steps 2 to 5. Repeat into each chain across.

 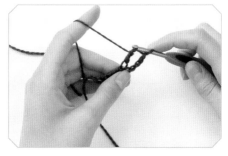 

2 Yarn over the hook and pull up a loop. There will be four loops on the hook.

4 Yarn over the hook and draw through two loops. There will be two loops on the hook.

6 To work the next row, make four chains and turn the work. Insert the hook into the second stitch (missing the first stitch because the four turning chains count as a stitch). Work under the top two loops and complete Steps 2 to 5. Continue across the row. Make the last stitch into the top chain of the previous row's turning chain.

Slip stitch (sl st)

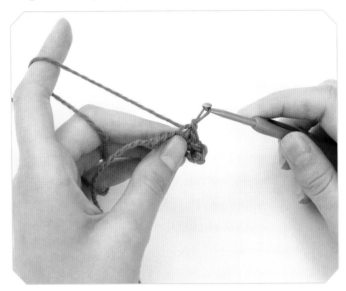

This stitch is rarely used to create crochet fabrics on its own. Instead it is used to join crochet fabrics together, work across a set of stitches without adding height, join rounds, or reinforce an edge.

To create a slip stitch in a foundation chain, insert the hook into the second chain from the hook. Yarn over the hook and draw it through the loop on the hook. To work the next row, turn the work without adding a turning chain and slip stitch into the first stitch of the row.

Working triple treble (trtr) and quadruple treble (qtr) crochet

Some patterns use the longer triple treble and even longer quadruple treble. These are worked in a similar manner to the treble crochet on the page 121. For the triple treble, yarn over the hook three times and draw through two loops each time until stitch is complete. For the quadruple treble, yarn over the hook four times and draw through two loops each time until stitch is complete.

Working into the front and back of stitches

Working around the post of a stitch creates decorative ridges and texture in the crocheted fabric. They are sometimes called relief or raised stitches.

FRONT POST DOUBLE CROCHET (FPTR)

1 Wrap the yarn around the hook and insert the hook from the front to the back of the fabric, taking it around the back of the post of the stitch. Bring it out at the front of the fabric. Yarn over the hook again and pull up a loop on the right side of the fabric (three loops on hook).

2 Yarn over the hook and draw it through the first two loops on the hook. Yarn over the hook again and draw it through the remaining two loops (one front post treble crochet made).

Back post double crochet (BPtr)

1 Wrap the yarn around the hook and insert the hook from the back to the front, taking it around the front of the post of the stitch and bring it out at the back of the crochet. Yarn over the hook again and pull up a loop on the wrong side of the fabric (three loops on hook).

3 Yarn over the hook again and draw it through the remaining two loops (one back post treble crochet made).

2 Yarn over the hook and draw it through the first two loops on the hook.

Increasing and Decreasing Stitches

Basic shaping is a simple matter of increasing and decreasing the number of stitches. These techniques are necessary for many crochet projects. Decrease stitches are worked over more than one stitch and combine several stitches in each stitch. The technique for a one-stitch decrease is shown below for each of the four basic crochet stitches.

To increase one or more stitches within a row or round

Work more than one stitch into a stitch of the previous row or round. Here the increase is shown in treble crochet, but the method is the same for all the other crochet stitches.

To increase several stitches at the beginning of a row

Work the number of turning chains required for the stitch plus an extra chain for each additional stitch you want to add. Miss the required number of turning chains and then work a stitch into the remaining chains to complete the increase.

To increase several stitches at the end of a row

1 Work extended stitches. For extended double crochet, insert the hook into the same stitch as the last double crochet of the row. *Pull up a loop, yarn over the hook, and draw through one loop only. Mark the chain stitch you have made.

2 Yarn over the hook and draw through the two loops on your hook to complete the stitch. Insert your hook into the marked chain and repeat from * to create the next stitch.

Double crochet decrease (dc2tog)

1 Insert the hook into the first stitch and pull up a loop. Insert the hook into the next stitch and pull up a loop. There will be three loops on the hook.

2 Yarn over the hook and draw through all three loops.

Half treble crochet decrease (htr2tog)

1 Yarn over the hook, insert the hook into the first stitch and pull up a loop. Yarn over the hook, insert the hook into the next stitch and pull up a loop. There will be five loops on the hook. For a less bulky half treble crochet decrease, omit this yarn over the hook.

2 Yarn over the hook and draw through all five loops.

Treble crochet decrease (tr2tog)

1 Yarn over the hook, insert the hook into the first stitch and pull up a loop. Yarn over the hook and draw through two loops on the hook. Yarn over the hook, insert the hook into the next stitch and pull up a loop. Yarn over the hook and draw through two loops. There will be three loops on the hook.

2 Yarn over the hook and draw through all three loops to complete the decrease.

Double Treble crochet decrease (dtr2tog)

1 This decrease is worked in a similar way to the treble crochet decrease. Work a double treble crochet into the first stitch until there are two loops on the hook, omitting the last step.

3 Yarn over the hook and draw through all three loops to complete the decrease.

2 Yarn over the hook twice, insert the hook into the next stitch and work a double treble crochet until three loops remain on the hook.

Working in the Round

Working crochet in the round is essential for motifs such as granny squares (see page 132). There are three methods of beginning a round and most patterns will have instructions for which method to use, but feel free to use a different method if none is suggested by the pattern.

Making a joined round of chains

This method is ideal if the first round has a large number of stitches, as it enables the stitches of the first round to lie flat without bunching or overlapping, but it will leave a hole in the centre of the fabric. You can also add additional chains to accommodate more stitches in the beginning round.

Creating a round of stitches by working into one chain

This method is easy to work but it is not a good choice if there are a large number of stitches in the first round as it will be overcrowded and the stitches will not lie flat. However it will give you a tight centre without a hole.

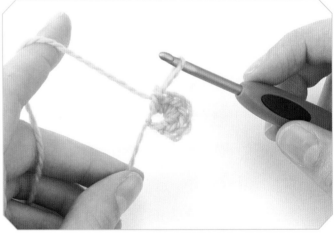

Make a short chain. Join the chain into a ring by making a slip stitch into the first chain. Work a turning chain (see page 117) to bring the round up to the height of the stitches, then work the first round of stitches into the ring. Work a slip stitch into the top chain of the turning chain to join the first round together.

For example, make two chains and work six double crochet stitches into the second chain from the hook. Work under the top loop only of the chain stitch as this will allow you to expand and tighten the chain as needed.

Magic loop

The magic loop or ring can be used to create a round with a tight centre and a lot of stitches. However, it is not suitable for slippery yarns because the yarn end may work loose.

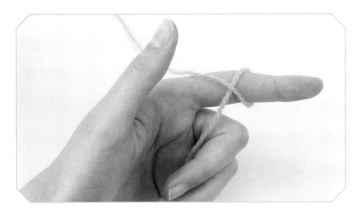

1 Wind the working yarn around your forefinger and cross it over the tail yarn, leaving a 15 cm (6 in.) tail.

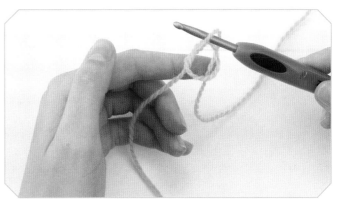

3 Insert the hook through the front of the loop, pull through a loop of the working yarn and hold it on the hook with your forefinger.

2 Slide the loop off your finger while pinching the X overlap you have made.

4 Yarn over the hook and work a chain stitch to secure. Crochet over both the magic loop and yarn tail as you complete the first round. Pull the yarn tail to tighten.

Working flat rounds

To keep crocheted fabric flat while working in rounds, work increase stitches evenly on each round.

1 Work a round of stitches and slip stitch into the first stitch to join it. Make a turning chain to bring the round to the correct height, but do not turn the work (unless instructed to do so in the pattern). The turning chain will count as a stitch. Work two stitches into each stitch of the previous round for Round 2.

2 For subsequent rounds, increase the stitch count by the same number of stitches as Round 1.

Working tubular rounds

1 Work a length of chain stitches equal to the diameter of the finished tube. Slip stitch into the first chain to join the round. Work a turning chain to bring the round up to height. Work one stitch into each chain, being careful not to twist the chain and join the round at the end. To create a straight seam, turn the work at the end of each round; otherwise, there will be a slanted seam.

2 Work the following rounds evenly (one stitch in each stitch). To create a tube with a closed end, work flat rounds to the diameter required for the tube to make the closed end, then work evenly until the tube is the desired height.

Joining in New Colours

Whether you need to join in a new colour of yarn at the beginning or in the middle of a row, the method is the same. Use the same technique for joining in a new ball of the same yarn colour, but note that this is best done at the beginning of a row.

1 Work the last stitch but stop at the last step before drawing through the final yarn over the hook. There will be two loops on the hook.

2 Drop the old colour behind the work and draw the new colour through to complete the stitch. Continue working with the colour as usual.

Granny Squares and Other Motifs

Granny squares are traditional crochet motifs usually created by working a series of rounds, increasing the number of stitches each time. The most common form uses treble crochet, but there are may other variations you can try. These motifs are quick and easy to make whether you're at home or out and about. They are also a great way to use up scraps of yarn and many crocheters find them more satisfying to work than row after row of stitches. Traditionally, each round of a motif is worked in a different colour, but you can also make single-colour motifs. They are also a great way to explore different colour combinations.

Joining motifs

Motifs can be joined together with sewn or crocheted seams and the seams can become part of the design. Align the stitches carefully before you start to join them. You may find it easiest to pin them together. Join irregular-shaped motifs using the 'join as you go' method described here by incorporating the joins into the last round of the second and each subsequent motif.

2 Continue to work the second motif in the established pattern up to the next chain 2 space, but do not chain 2. Repeat Steps 1 and 2 for the next join.

1 For example, chain 1, then insert the hook from front to back into any chain 2 space of the first motif. Work a slip stitch and chain 1 to complete the join.

3 Complete the final round of the second motif as established in the pattern. Add more motifs until you have the desired length.

Finishing your Work

Finishing

When you have worked your last stitch, you need to cut the yarn and fasten off. Do not cut the yarn too close to the stitches – about 15 cm (6 in.) will leave you enough to weave into the stitches to secure it.

1 Cut the yarn, wrap it around the hook and pull it through the last stitch on the hook.

2 Pull the yarn tail tight to fasten off, then weave in.

Weaving in ends

The final instructions of any crochet pattern usually include the words 'weave in the loose ends.' On a project with many colours this may seem time-confusing, but it is essential for a neat, professional finish.

The best tool for the job is a tapestry needle with a large eye and blunt tip. Thread the yarn tail onto it and, working on the wrong side of the fabric, pull the yarn through at least 5 cm (2 in.) of stitches, making sure the needle goes through the loops of the stitches and not the yarn itself. Then weave it back in the opposite direction for 2.5 cm (1 in.) to prevent the end from working loose.

Blocking

Blocking a piece of crochet before using it or sewing it to other pieces to create an item of clothing creates a neat finish and makes sewing seams much easier. It means that the final pieces will be the correct size and the stitches will be shown to the best advantage.

There are two methods you can use: cold water and steam. Cold water blocking is used for synthetic man-made yarns, such as acrylic and nylon yarns that would be damaged by the heat of steam blocking. Pin the crochet to the correct size on a folded towel or ironing board with the right side facing up. Spray with cold water to dampen it, but do not over-saturate it and allow it to dry completely before removing the pins.

Steam blocking is only suitable for natural fibres, such as wool and cotton. Place the iron over the piece and allow the steam to set the stitches. Never press the iron directly onto the piece being blocked, because this will flatten and distort the stitches.

Seams and Joining

Take time when sewing your crochet sections together so that the finished item is neat and reflects the time you have taken to create it. There are several ways to join seams and you can use more than one method in a project if you wish. If you want a hidden seam, then mattress stitch is a good choice. Use the same yarn you used to crochet the item. If you want the seam to become part of the finished design, choose a slip stitch or a double crochet seam. You could also use a contrasting colour yarn to add decorative detail.

Mattress stitch

This seam has no bulk and it is used frequently in garment construction. Place the crocheted pieces on a flat surface with the right sides facing up, making sure the stitches are aligned. Insert the needle through the post of the bottom right stitch, cross over to the corresponding left stitch and at the same time draw the yarn through the post of the stitch. Continue working backward and forward through the posts of the stitches. Gently tighten the seam while you work, but don't make it too tight.

Top seams

Top seams can be joined with double crochet (see page 118) or slip stitches (see page 122). Slip stitch creates a flat seam but it will not have as much stretch as a single crochet seam.

SLIP STITCH SEAM

Hold the two pieces of crochet to be joined with right sides facing each other. Insert the hook through the first stitch of both pieces and the pull yarn through to make a slip stitch. Insert the hook through the next stitch of both pieces, yarn over the hook and pull the yarn through both the stitches and the loop on the hook. Continue to the end of the seam.

DOUBLE CROCHET SEAM

Work in the same way as slip stitch, using Double crochet.

Whip stitch

This stitch is quick to work and is especially useful on straight-edged fabrics. It's a good choice for joining motifs together. With the right sides of the fabric pieces held together, insert the needle from the front to the back of a stitch and through the corresponding stitch on the other piece. Bring the needle to the front again and repeat until the seam is finished

Back stitch

This sturdy seam has some bulk to it, so test it first to see if it's an appropriate seam for your crocheted fabric. With the right sides of the fabric pieces held together and working about one stitch space away from the edge of the fabric, insert the needle from the back to the front through both thicknesses. Insert the needle from the front to the back of the fabric and then bring it up through to the front again one stitch beyond the working yarn. For the next stitch, insert the needle from the front to the back in the same place as the last stitch ended and again bring the needle to the front one stitch beyond the working yarn. Repeat until the seam is finished.

Reading Patterns

Crochet patterns are a step-by-step guide to creating a finished item. They usually include information about the materials, tension, measurements, or finished size, as well as step-by-step instructions and abbreviations. Some also include colour charts that offer a visual representation of the pattern.

Punctuation

Patterns are a concise and easy-to-read set of instructions that use abbreviations and punctuation to help avoid needless repetition. Once you understand them you will find following the pattern becomes automatic.

( ) ROUND BRACKETS give additional information about a pattern. For example (12dc) listed at the end of a row says that you should have 12 double crochet stitches when the row has been completed.

CH 3 (COUNTS AS FIRST TR) explains that the three turning chains count as a treble crochet stitch and the stitch is included in the instructions for the stitch count at the end of the row or round.

[ ] SQUARE BRACKETS designate a set of stitch instructions, such as [1tr, ch3, 1tr]. This means that you will treble crochet, chain 3, treble crochet all in the same stitch.

It may also contain a stitch repeat – [1tr, ch3, 1tr] twice. For this, you will treble crochet, chain 3, treble crochet all in the same stitch twice.

* AN ASTERISK indicates stitch instructions and pattern repeats on a row or round. *1tr, ch1, miss next st. Rep from * 4 times to last st, 1tr. This instruction tells you to treble crochet, chain 1, miss the next stitch. Repeat four times and then treble crochet into the last stitch.

Colour charts

Colour charts may be a complete chart or a section that represents colour placement. Each stitch is represented by a square, so written instructions are not always necessary (although some patterns may give both written and charted instructions). A legend to the symbols will be given with the chart.

The crochet patterns in this book have been given a skill level to help you to determine the complexity of the designs. See page 139 for more information.

Skill Level key

✳ ✳ ✳ ✳ EXPERIENCED

✳ ✳ ✳ INTERMEDIATE

✳ ✳ EASY

✳ BEGINNER

Abbreviations

The patterns in this book feature a number of standard abbreviations, which are explained below. These abbreviations are logical and easy to understand. Any abbreviations that are exclusive to one pattern are listed and explained with that pattern.

beg	beginning	**MC**	main colour
blo	back loop only	**meas**	measures
BP	back post	**rem**	remaining
CC	contrasting colour	**rep**	repeat
ch	chain	**RS**	right side
cl	cluster	**qtr**	quadruple treble
dc	double crochet	**sl st**	slip stitch
dtr	double treble crochet	**sp(s)**	space(s)
dtr2tog	double treble next 2sts together	**st(s)**	stitches
		tch	turning chain
dtr3tog	double treble next 3sts together	**tr**	treble crochet
		tr2tog	treble crochet next 2sts together
flo	front loop only		
foll	following	**tr3tog**	treble crochet next 3sts together
FPtr	front post treble crochet		
FPdtr	front post double treble crochet	**trtr**	triple treble
gr	group	**WS**	wrong side
htr	half treble	**yoh**	yarn over hook
htr2tog	half treble next 2sts together		

Useful Information

YARN WEIGHTS

Yarn-Weight Symbol and Category Name	**1** Super Fine	**2** Fine	**3** Light	**4** Medium	**5** Bulky	**6** Super Bulky
Types of Yarn in Category	Sock, Fingering, Baby	Sport, Baby	DK, Light Worsted	Worsted, Afghan, Aran	Chunky, Craft, Rug	Bulky, Roving
Crochet Tension Ranges* in Double Crochet to 10 cm	21 to 32sts	16 to 20sts	12 to 17sts	11 to 14sts	8 to 11sts	5 to 9sts
Recommended Hook in Metric Size Range	2.25 to 3.5 mm	3.5 to 4.5 mm	4.5 to 5.5 mm	5.5 to 6.5 mm	6.5 to 9 mm	9 mm and larger
Recommended Hook in US Size Range	B-1 to E-4	E-4 to 7	7 to I-9	I-9 to K-10½	K-10½ to M-13	M-13 and larger

These are guidelines only. The above reflect the most commonly used tensions and needle or hook sizes for specific yarn categories.

Crochet Hook Sizes

Millimetre	US Size*
2.25 mm	B-1
2.75 mm	C-2
3.25 mm	D-3
3.5 mm	E-4
3.75 mm	F-5
4 mm	G-6
4.5 mm	7
5 mm	H-8
5.5 mm	I-9
6 mm	J-10
6.5 mm	K-10½
8 mm	L-11
9 mm	M/N-13
10 mm	N/P-15

Letter or number may vary. Rely on the millimetre sizing.

Steel Hook Sizes

Millimetre	US Size*
2.75 mm	1
2.25 mm	2
1.65 mm	7

Metric Conversions

Yards x .91 = metres
Metres x 1.09 = yards
Ounces x 28.35 = grams
Grams x .035 = ounces

Skill Levels

Each project has been given a skill-level rating.

❀ Beginner: Projects for first-time crocheters using basic stitches; minimal shaping.

❀❀ Easy: Projects using yarn with basic stitches, repetitive stitch patterns, simple colour changes and simple shaping and finishing.

❀❀❀ Intermediate: Projects using a variety of techniques, such as basic lace patterns or colour patterns; mid-level shaping and finishing.

❀❀❀❀ Experienced: Projects with intricate stitch patterns, techniques and dimension, such as non-repeating patterns, multicolour techniques, fine threads, small hooks, detailed shaping and refined finishing.

Yarns Used in the Projects

Vintage Fan Ripple Blanket

Scheepjeswol Softfun; 60% cotton
40% acrylic, 50 g/1.76 oz, 140 m/153 yds.
2 balls in each colour: CCa sh2531 Olive,
CCb 2 sh2514 Rose, CCc sh2466 Skin,
CCd sh2449 Coral, CCe sh2519 Violet, CCf
sh2496 Soft Yellow, CCg sh2432 Light Blue.

Annie Blanket

Drops Muskat DK; 100% cotton, 50 g/
1.76 oz, 100 m/109 yds.
MC 5 balls in sh18 White scraps in the
following colours for the stripes: Denim Blue,
Light Olive, Light Pink, Vanilla Yellow, Light
Blue Purple, Bordeaux, Ice Blue, Rust, Silver
Green, Wine, Dark Orange, Peach.

Daisy Baby Blanket

Rosarios4 Regata; 100% cotton 100 g/
3.5 oz, 273 m/ 299 yds.
MC 2 balls in sh01 Cream, 1 ball in each
contrasting colour: CCa sh25 Orange, CCb
sh29 Light Orange, CCc sh33 Yellow, CCd
sh61 Light Pink, CCe sh50 Dark Pink, CCf
sh99 Purple, CCg sh03 Beige, CCh sh102
Green.

Colour Wheel Hexagon Blanket

Drops Safran; 100% cotton, 50 g/1.76 oz,
160 m/175 yds.
MC 16 balls in 17 White, approx 25 g/1 oz.
each of 24 additional colours.

Happy Colours Blanket

Drops Safran; 100% cotton, 50 g/1.76 oz,
160 m/ 175 yds.
MC 15 x balls in sh 17 White, 800 g /29 oz.
in total of other colours.

Flower Power Runner

Drops Paris; 100% cotton yarn, 50 g/1.76 oz,
75 m/83 yds.
MC 1 ball in sh35 Vanilla, scraps of
15 contrast colours.

Star Fruit Rug

Stitch Nation Full O' Sheep; 100% Peruvian
Wool, 100 g/4 oz, 142 m/155 yds.
1 skein in each colour: CCa Poppy, CCb
Clementine, CCc Honeycomb, CCd
Meadow, CCe Thyme, CCf Aquamarine,
CCg Mediterranean, CCh Peony, CCi
Plummy.

Large Granny-Square Pillow

Phildar Phil Coton 3; 100% cotton,
50 g/1.76 oz, 121 m/132 yds.
1 ball each in 8 contrast colours.

Sunflower Motif Pillow

King Cole Bamboo Cotton; 50% cotton
50% bamboo, 100 g /3.5 oz, 230 m/250 yds.
MC 1 ball in sh 538 Cream, scraps in
4 colours.

Chevron Pillow

Drops Paris; 100% cotton 50 g/1.76 oz,
75 m/83 yds.
MC 5 balls in sh17 Off White, 1 ball in
each contrasting colour: sh41 Mustard, sh35
Vanilla, sh46 Rust, sh32 Light Blue Purple,
sh102 Spray Blue, sh26 Dark Beige, sh59
Light Old Pink, sh25 Moss Green.

Round Floor Pillow

Phildar Phil Coton 3; 100% cotton,
50 g/1.76 oz, 121 m/132 yds.
1 ball each in 7 colours.

Spoke Mandala

Drops Paris; 100% cotton, 50 g/1.76 oz,
75 m/83 yds.
Scraps in 8 colours.

Picot-Edge Mandala

Drops Paris; 100% cotton, 50 g/1.76 oz,
75 m/83 yds.
Scraps in 12 colours.

Mandala Stool Cover

Red Heart Stitch Nation Washable Ewe;
100% superwash wool, 100 g/3.5 oz,
167 m/183 yds.
1 skein in each colour: CCa sh3652 Clover,
CCb sh3711 Icing, CCc sh3525 Dragonfly,
CCd sh3501 Robin's Egg, CCe sh3215
Duckling, CCf sh3706 Zinnia, CCg sh3582
Lilac.
Red Heart Stitch Nation Bamboo Ewe;
55% viscose bamboo, 45% wool, 100 g/3½ oz,
162 m/177 yds.
CCh 1 skein in sh 5625 Sprout.
Paton's Classic Wool; 100% wool, 100 g/
3½ oz, 192 m/210 yds.
1 skein in each colour: CCi sh77404 Orchid,
CCj sh77253 Burnt Orange, CCk sh77132
Royal Blue.
Lion Brand Wool Ease; 80% acrylic,
20% wool, 85 g/3 oz, 180 m/197 yds.
CCl 1 skein in sh191 Violet.
Lion Brand Pound of Love; 100% acrylic,
448 g/16 oz, 932 m/1,020 yds.
CCm 1 skein in Antique White.

Heart and Flower Motifs

Annell Cotton 8; 100% cotton, 50 g/1.76 oz,
170 m/186 yds.
Scraps in several colours.

Crocheted Christmas Baubles

Rico Essentials Cotton; 100% cotton, 50 g/1.76 oz, 130 m/142 yds.
Scraps in 4 colours.

Butterfly Pot Holders

Scheepjeswol Softfun; 60% cotton 40% acrylic, 50 g/1.76 oz, 140 m/ 153 yds.
Scraps in 7 colours.

Lace Crochet Coasters

Drops Paris; 100% cotton, 50 g/1.76 oz, 75 m/83 yds.
1 ball each in 6 graduated colours.
Annell Cotton 8; 100% cotton, 50 g/1.76 oz, 170 m/186 yds.
1 ball for edging.

Breakfast Cosy Set

Rico Creative Cotton; 100% cotton, 50 g/1.76 oz, 85 m/93 yds.
Scraps in 5 colours.

Drops of Colour Headband

Drops Paris; 100% cotton, 50 g/1.76 oz, 75 m/83 yds.
Scraps in sh35 Vanilla, sh41 Mustard, sh14 Strong Yellow, sh38 Raspberry, sh37 Rusty Red, sh42 Army, sh44 Brown.

Floral Hair Grips

Annell Cotton 8; 100% cotton, 50 g/1.76 oz, 170 m/185 yds.
A selection of colours.

Rainbow Wrist Cuffs

Debbie Bliss Baby Cashmerino; 55% wool 33% acrylic 12% cashmere, 50 g/1.76 oz, 125 m/136 yds.
1 ball in each colour: MC sh026 Duck Egg, CCa sh034 Red, CCb sh006 Candy Pink, CCc sh204 Baby Blue, CCd sh071 Royal, CCe sh006 Amber, CCf sh608 Pale Lilac, CCg sh059 Mallard, CCh sh018 Citrus.

Slouch Hat

TreLiz chunky; 100% baby alpaca yarn, 100 g/3½ oz, 100 m/109 yds.
1 skein in Orange Pink Orchid.

Dancing Hearts Wrap

Anne Geddes Baby acrylic sportweight yarn by Red Heart Yarns; 100 g/3.5 oz, 311 m/340 yds.
1 ball in each colour: MC sh100 Lilly, CCa sh623 Spearmint, CCb sh691 Grass, CCc sh702 Rosie, CCd sh763 Taffy.

Wildflowers Scarf

Katia Merino; 100% wool, 50 g/1.76 oz, 102 m/111 yds. or Rico Design Essentials Cotton DK; 50 g/1.76 oz, 130 m/142 yds. 175 g/6 oz. in total.

Ombré String Cowl

Lion Brand Vanna's Choice; 100% acrylic, 100 g/3.5 oz, 156 m/170 yds.
Scraps in MC sh141 Wild Berry, CCa sh144 Magenta, CCb sh143 Antique Rose, CCc sh142 Rose, CCd sh138 Pink Poodle (approx 137 m/150 yds. in total).

Blossom Necklace

Debbie Bliss Rialto 4 ply; 100% extra fine merino wool, 50 g/1.76 oz, 180 m/197 yds. or DMC Natura Just Cotton; 100% cotton, 50 g/1.76 oz, 155 m/170 yds.
Scraps in several colours.

Granny-Square Clutch Bag

Phildar Phil coton 3; 100% cotton, 50 g/ 1.76 oz, 121 m/132 yds.
MC 1 ball in 010 Blanc, scraps in 8 colours.

Mobile phone and Tablet Covers

Sirdar Snuggly DK; 45% acrylic, 55% nylon, 50 g/1.76 oz, 165 m/179 yds.
1 ball in each colour: CCa sh0252 Lemon, CCb sh0403 Wobble, CCc sh0420 Lolly, CCd sh0242 Flamenco, CCf sh0439 Little Bud, CCd sh0440 Blue Bud, CCg sh0441 Little Bow.

Star Backpack

Phildar Cotton Phil 3; 100% cotton, 50 g/1.76 oz, 121 m/132 yds. or Schachemayr Catania; 100% cotton 50 g/1.76 oz, 125 m/137 yds.
1 ball each in 14 contrast colours.

The Weekender Bag

Lion Brand Vanna's Choice worsted weight yarn; 100% acrylic, 100g/3.5 oz, 156 m/170 yds.
Small Bag MC 2 balls in sh 305 Pearl Mist, 1 ball in each contrasting colour: CC1 130 Honey, CC2 158 Mustard. Large Bag MC 2 balls in sh 305 Pearl Mist, 1 ball in each contrasting colour: CC1 sh135 Rust, CC2 sh134 Terra Cotta.

Index

A

abbreviations — 137
Annie Blanket — 10, 16–17, 140
Astle, Amy — 8

B

Back Pack, Star — 11, 100–103, 141
back post treble crochet (BPtr) — 123
back stitch — 135
Bag, Weekender — 11, 104–109, 141
Baubles, Crocheted Christmas — 11, 60–61, 141
Benthem, Annemarie — 8
blankets
　Annie Blanket — 10, 16–17, 140
　Colour Wheel Hexagon Blanket — 10, 140
　Daisy Baby Blanket — 10, 18–21, 140
　Happy Colours Blanket — 10, 24–27, 140
　Vintage Fan Ripple Blanket — 10, 14–15, 140
blocking — 133
Blossom Necklace — 11, 92–93, 141
Bramham, Ruth — 9
Breakfast Cosy Set — 11, 68–71, 141
Butterfly Pot Holders — 11, 62–65, 141

C

Campbell, Ali — 8
Carlson, Susan — 9
chains — 116
　creating round of stitches by working into one chain — 128
　foundation chain — 116
　making joined round of chains — 128
　turning chains — 117
　working into the chain — 117
Chevron Pillow — 10, 38–40, 140
Christmas Baubles, Crocheted — 11, 60–61, 141
Clutch Bag, Granny Square — 11, 94–95, 141
Coasters, Lace Crochet — 11, 66–67, 141
Colour Wheel Hexagon Blanket — 10, 22–23, 140

colour
　colour charts — 136
　joining in new colours — 131
Cowl, Ombré String — 11, 90–91, 141
Cosy Set, Breakfast — 11, 68–71, 141
crochet hooks — 112, 139
crochet techniques — 111
　back post treble crochet (BPtr) — 123
　blocking — 133
　creating round of stitches by working into one chain — 128
　decreases — 126–127
　double crochet (dc) — 118
　double treble crochet (dtr) — 121
　finishing — 133
　foundation chain and chain stitches — 116
　half treble crochet (htr) — 119
　holding the hook and yarn — 114
　increases — 124–125
　joining in new colours — 131
　joining motifs — 132
　magic loop — 129
　making joined round of chains — 128
　making slip knot — 116
　quadruple treble crochet (qtr) — 122
　seams and joining — 134–135
　slip stitch (sl st) — 122
　tension — 115
　treble crochet (tr) — 120
　triple treble crochet (trtr) — 122
　turning chains — 117
　weaving in ends — 133
　working flat rounds — 130
　working into front and back of stitches — 122
　working into the chain — 117
　working tubular rounds — 130
Crocheted Christmas Baubles — 11, 60–61, 141

D

Daisy Baby Blanket — 10, 18–21, 140
Daisy Motif — 57–58
Dancing Hearts Wrap — 11, 85–87, 141

decreases — 126–127
　double crochet decrease (dc2tog) — 125
　double treble crochet decrease (dtr2tog) — 127
　half treble crochet decrease (htr2tog) — 126
　treble crochet decrease (tr2tog) — 126
double crochet (dc) — 118
　double crochet decrease (dc2tog) — 125
double treble crochet (dtr) — 121
　double treble crochet decrease (dtr2tog) — 127
Drops of Colour Headband — 11, 74–75, 141
Dudek, Sara — 9

F

finishing — 133
　weaving in ends — 133
flowers — 56–59
　Blossom Necklace — 11, 92–93, 141
　Floral Hair Grips — 11, 76–77, 141
　Flower Power Runner — 10, 28–29, 140
　Wildflowers Scarf — 11, 88–89, 141

G

granny squares — 132
　Granny-Square Clutch Bag — 11, 94–95, 141
　Large Granny-Square Pillow — 10, 34–35, 140

H

Hair Grips, Floral — 11, 76–77, 141
half treble crochet (htr) — 119
　half treble crochet decrease (htr2tog) — 126
Happy Colours Blanket — 10, 24–27, 140
Hat, Slouch — 11, 82–84, 141
Headband, Drops of Colour — 11, 74–75, 141
hearts
　Dancing Hearts Wrap — 11, 85–87, 141
　Heart and Flower Motifs — 10, 56–59, 140
Heffernan, Carmen — 8
Hollewijn, Dorien — 9

I

increases 124–125
  increasing one or more stitches within row
    or round 124
  increasing several stitches at beginning
    of row 124
  increasing several stitches at end of row 125

J

joining 134–135
  joining motifs 132
Joy, Ruthie 9

L

Lace Crochet Coasters 11, 66–67, 141
Large Granny Square Pillow 10, 34–35, 140
Little Doolally 8

M

Made by Do 9
magic loop 129
mandalas
  Butterfly 62–65
  Mandala Stool Cover 10, 50–55, 140
  Picot-Edge Mandala 10, 47–49, 140
  Spoke Mandala 10, 44–46, 140
mattress stitch 134
metric conversions 139
Mobile phone and
  Tablet Covers 11, 96–99, 141

N

Necklace, Blossom 11, 92–93, 141

O

Ombré String Cowl 11, 90–91, 141

P

patterns, reading 136–137
  abbreviations 137
  colour charts 136
  punctuation 136
Paul, Sandra 9
Picot-Edge Mandala 10, 47–49, 140
pillows
  Chevron Pillow 10, 38–40, 140
  Large Granny Square Pillow 10, 34–35, 140
  Round Floor Pillow 10, 41–43, 140
  Sunflower Motif Pillow 10, 36–37, 140
Pot Holders, Butterfly 11, 62–65, 141

Q

quadruple treble crochet (qtr) 122

R

Rainbow Wrist Cuffs 11, 78–81, 141
Round Floor Pillow 10, 41–43, 140
rounds 128–129
  working flat rounds 130
  working tubular rounds 130
Rug, Star Fruit 10, 30–33, 140
Runner, Flower Power 10, 28–29, 140

S

Scarf, Wildflowers 11, 88–89, 141
seams 134–135
  double crochet seam 134
  slip stitch seam 134
Seven-Petal Flower Motif 58
skill levels 139
slip stitch (sl st) 122
  slip stitch seam 134
slip knot 116
Slouch Hat 11, 82–84, 141
Slump, Marinke 8
Spoke Mandala 10, 44–46, 140
Star Backpack 11, 100–103, 141
Star Fruit Rug 10, 30–33, 140
Sunflower Motif Pillow 10, 36–37, 140

T

Tablet Cover 11, 96–99, 141
tools 112–113
treble crochet (tr) 120
tension 115
triple treble crochet (trtr) 122

U

Useful Information 139

V

Vintage Fan Ripple Blanket 10, 14–15, 140

W

Weekender Bag, The 11, 104–109, 141
whip stitch 135
Wildflowers Scarf 11, 88–89, 141
Wrap, Dancing Hearts 11, 85–87, 141
Wrist Cuffs, Rainbow 11, 78–81, 141

Y

yarn 112, 139, 140–141

Acknowledgements

The publishers would like to thank Marinke Slump for providing the inspiration for this book and all those who contributed their beautiful designs: Amy Astle, Annemarie Benthem, Ruth Bramham, Ali Campbell, Susan Carlson, Sara Dudek, Carmen Heffernan, Dorien Hollewijn and Sandra Paul.